T0128125

THANKS FOR TELLING HER
"NO"

RUTH DAVENPORT

WESTBOW
PRESS®
A DIVISION OF THOMAS NELSON
& ZONDERVAN

Copyright © 2023 Ruth Davenport.

All rights reserved. No part of this book may be used or reproduced by any means, graphic, electronic, or mechanical, including photocopying, recording, taping or by any information storage retrieval system without the written permission of the author except in the case of brief quotations embodied in critical articles and reviews.

This book is a work of non-fiction. Unless otherwise noted, the author and the publisher make no explicit guarantees as to the accuracy of the information contained in this book and in some cases, names of people and places have been altered to protect their privacy.

WestBow Press books may be ordered through booksellers or by contacting:

WestBow Press
A Division of Thomas Nelson & Zondervan
1663 Liberty Drive
Bloomington, IN 47403
www.westbowpress.com
844-714-3454

Because of the dynamic nature of the Internet, any web addresses or links contained in this book may have changed since publication and may no longer be valid. The views expressed in this work are solely those of the author and do not necessarily reflect the views of the publisher, and the publisher hereby disclaims any responsibility for them.

Any people depicted in stock imagery provided by Getty Images are models, and such images are being used for illustrative purposes only. Certain stock imagery © Getty Images.

Scripture quotations are taken from the Holy Bible, New Living Translation, Copyright © 1996, 2004, 2015 by Tyndale House Foundation. Used by permission of Tyndale House Publishers, Inc., Carol Stream, Illinois 60188. All rights reserved.

ISBN: 978-1-9736-9995-8 (sc)
ISBN: 978-1-9736-9996-5 (hc)
ISBN: 978-1-9736-9994-1 (e)

Library of Congress Control Number: 2023911038

Print information available on the last page.

WestBow Press rev. date: 9/25/2023

CONTENTS

DEDICATION

This book is dedicated mainly to Shelbi. She is truly my special gift from God. She is my inspiration. Also to Ronald, I would have never started or finished this without your persistence and total faith in me. Thank you for seeing in me what I could not. Thank you for believing in the importance of telling this story. Thank you, Ashley, Kari, Jeremy, Daniel, Lydia, Landon, Logan, and Samuel. Thank you for your patience and willingness to allow me so much time with Shelbi. I know it has not always been easy, but each of you have provided comfort, peace and laughter as we journeyed through this life.

FOREWORD

Adventures with Shelbi

I am so fortunate to have Shelbi in my life. I have the distinct honor of following in her footsteps, trying to keep up with her accomplishments I have come to realize that I will always be a few steps behind her. I know now that she is my teacher and mentor and that our roles over the years have shifted. Her presence is powerful. She is kind even to people who do not understand her gifts and talents. She is patient with professionals who have difficulty understanding that they are not in charge nor are they the experts. Shelbi's lived experience is more extensive than any academic professor, an executive manager, any powerful paid advocate. Shelbi is the example of the future for people with labels, people who have been defined by their disabilities, people who have been diminished because of difference. I have known Shelbi for eight years. I was one of her teachers and manager when she was a part of a post-secondary certificate program for people with disabilities at Texas A&M University. I remember how committed and responsible she was. She was also shy...at least from my perspective. She isn't shy anymore. She graduated from the Texas A&M program at the top of her class. I recruited her to pursue certification as a People Planning Together trainer, a peer-to-peer training for people with disabilities presented by people with disabilities. She was the first person in Texas to receive this certification. In fact, she was instrumental in revising the curriculum to be more person centered. Shelbi would co-train with me at A&M. Our audience was young people with disabilities. I would present my part of the training and the students were polite and respectful. But when Shelbi began to teach the students were on the edge of their seats, mesmerized by Shelbi's presentation. I believe the students saw Shelbi as an example of who they could be. She was a person with similar lived experiences, someone who had been told they couldn't go to college, a person with shared experiences of others who had power over them. Shared oppression. When I saw what was happening in the room, I knew who the real teacher was. Not me. Shelbi would always be the lead teacher and I would try to support her as best as I could. Shelbi has achieved so much at such an early age. She had a vision of graduating from Texas A&M University. She had so many hoops to get through. So often she was told no or diminished because of her disability. It is hard to fathom how many barriers she encountered as she achieved one milestone after another. These accomplishments are difficult for anyone to achieve. And everyone, disability or not needs supports. Nothing was handed to her. She earned these accomplishments with the support of her mom, family, and other people in her life. I wonder how many times she was knocked down because people perceived she didn't belong. She always got up, got up, got up. I'll never know how often. She would keep them to herself or share them with her biggest fan, her mom. Shelbi is kind. She is direct with what she has to say, so, she will be heard. She had been told she didn't belong, told by people who should support her how to do her job, people who struggle with the realization that Shelbi is the expert, and they aren't. People who fear what they don't understand. Shelbi has a streamed show with guests with lived experiences and leaders in the peer-to-peer movement. Her voice is being heard by many, many people. I have often wondered how many people with disability labels listen and watch her and are struck with the realization that they belong; they are valued, and dreams do happen with hard work and tenacity. Shelbi has many, many more adventures ahead. Her accomplishments will be amazing. Most of all her voice may reach a person with a disability from a small town in Texas who will think... maybe just maybe I can dream again. She did, so I can.

Jeff Garrison-Tate, CEO/Owner Better Lives
Mentor Trainer, The Learning Community on Person Centered Practices.

I can do everything through
Christ who gives me strength!

—Philippians 4:13 (NLT)

PROLOGUE

The story you are about to read is truly unique, not because Shelbi faced many hardships. Her life is a blessing due to the hardships. Each chapter of this book is titled with a particular name for God. These names became real for Shelbi and me as we ventured through our lives. She is only twenty-six years old at the time of this writing. She has experienced God's undying faithfulness in ways many of us never will. Because of her life experiences, I, too, experienced God's careful guidance and undying love in a very real way.

The chapters will conclude with short messages from Shelbi. She shares her memories and thoughts of how her disability affected her daily life. You will see that our views differ about what was happening in her life. I seemed to be a more defensive "mama bear"; she was loving life, almost oblivious to what was taking place. This does not mean that she did not feel pain and frustration. She felt deeply but was able to see the good more quickly than I could.

This is a book written through my eyes. I am her mom. Sharing Shelbi's story is meant to be an encouragement when you face difficulties. It is written to all members of the family surrounding a loved one who struggles with daily living. You need to know you are never alone; even when you feel isolated, God is with you, and people around you are available. My two older daughters were already nine and twelve when Shelbi was born. Ashley and Kari were a huge help in raising her. She often tells people she had three moms. The final chapter is completely about many of the people who have been, and continue to, pour into Shelbi's life. You will find thoughts and letters from her family and friends. These are meant to touch those family members who are facing the daily struggles and blessings of living with a relative who has special needs. These needs are not always physical. Many needs are met through supporting the individual emotionally and allowing them to live their best life. I am also including some notes from people who have made a difference in her life. I want her to be able to read these notes when she feels discouraged. I want her to know the many lives she touched and remind her there are more to come. I am sure I left out some people who made a huge difference in her life. She knows who you are, and so do I.

All of us face hardships throughout our lives. How we deal with these hardships is what creates the next steps in our lives. I made many mistakes and asked God lots of questions. I continue to do the same. It is good to ask when we do not understand. The hard part is accepting the answers to those questions. During many instances, I found myself telling God what the answer should be. This just led to more frustration and pain. The more I let God have full control of Shelbi's life, the easier it was to see the wonderful life she leads. The verse you see at the beginning of this prologue is her life's verse. She knows she can do anything she puts her mind to, and God will give her the strength to figure it out. This does not mean it will be easy. Shelbi and I both know that much of what she accomplished in life occurred through major difficulties. The rewards came through the outcomes. Some rewards will never be known. The road we have been down and are continuing to travel is filled with many ups and many, many downs. As we continue to journey, I am excited and cautiously aware that more obstacles will come. More walls will go up. More people will speak negative thoughts into Shelbi's life. What I know now is that she will survive. We will work together, or independently, to meet each new adventure with determination and even a little excitement. We know God has something ahead for both of us to learn from and experience.

Shelbi dedicates her life to giving back. She wants all people, not just people with disabilities, to live life to the fullest. She is certain that each of you have your own story, but some of you cannot express what you are feeling. I am praying that you can use her testimony and find God all around you in every situation. I want to encourage you to keep trying. Find a way to do what you want to do. Remember, God loves you and cares for each part of your life. Shelbi does too. She loves deeply and constantly. I hope you enjoy this book.

1

THE GREAT
PHYSICIAN

Yes, you have been with me from birth;
from my mother's womb you have cared for me.
No wonder I am always praising you!

—PSALM 71:6 (NLT)

I n the beginning, God. The simplicity and complexity of that statement sets the stage for the story you are about to read. It sets the stage for each life, but Shelbi's life was given to me. She is my youngest daughter, and her life changed my life in ways I would have never chosen, much less imagined. My dad was a Baptist preacher, and a chaplain in the air force. As a child, our family traveled to many different cities and states, and even to Turkey. I loved traveling. I still do. The joys of engaging in new adventures, meeting new friends, and seeing the world make my heart happy. When I was beginning my freshman year of high school, Daddy was called to preach at the First Baptist Church in a very small Texas town. The next four years were a whirlwind of education, sports, and living life. I married my high school sweetheart when I was nineteen years old. After graduating from Texas A&M University, I started teaching in my hometown. This school district would become the only one I ever worked for. I continued teaching, became principal, and retired after thirty-two years.

I tell you all this to let you know where I was when Shelbi entered my life. I was the elementary school principal. I had been teaching fifth grade for the past eleven years. I loved teaching. The opportunity to open children's minds to so many things was extremely rewarding. Each year was unique due to the changes in personalities of all the various students. My husband and I were the parents of two beautiful girls. Ashley, the oldest, was twelve years old. She had just started junior-high sports and loved every bit of it. Kari was nine years old. She was a student at the same elementary school where I taught. They were both amazing students. Raising them was easy. While I was still part of their daily lives, they were very independent.

I remember the day I found out I was pregnant with Shelbi. Ronald and I were completely surprised. Having another child was not in our five or even ten-year plan. We were both working and busy raising the girls. I had just completed my master's degree at Texas A&M. We told Ashley and Kari about the baby on the way home from one of Ashley's games. They were thrilled. We were all eager to have a baby in the house.

God was with us from the beginning. The instant Shelbi was conceived and forming in my womb, He knew who she was. Her family was ready for her. It was a cold February morning. She was almost a Valentine's baby, missing it by one day. I was thirty-four years old when Shelbi entered this world. I was already planning her little life out. I could see her following in her sisters' footsteps. She would make good grades, play sports, cheerlead, and enjoy traveling. Having semisuccessfully raised two other wonderful daughters, this would be a breeze. I learned from Ashley and Kari. Shelbi's life would be different, easier, since I knew what I was doing. Little did I know God had a completely different plan.

We live in a small town about forty-five minutes from the hospital. In order for Ashley and Kari to not be alone in the hospital, we picked up my niece to go with us. I was having labor pains about every four minutes as we made the drive to the big city. Shelbi's sisters sat in silence in the back seat, awaiting the end of this long nine months. I was ready for an epidural when I walked on the floor, but of course, that did not happen. The girls walked with me for hours as Shelbi took her time getting in position to enter this world. They were not able to stay in the delivery room due to some complications I had with my blood pressure. I did not get to see their expressions when they found out it was Shelbi and not Robert Tyler. That was the boy's name her dad and I chose twelve years ago when Ashley was born. We were pretty sure this was going to be our son, but God knew better.

He sent us a gift that only He could give. Shelbi was born at about nine in the morning with hardly any hair and bound to be content with life. From the day we took her home, she showed great endurance. She slept through the night and loved being talked to and cared for by her sisters. Shelbi stole our hearts from the first time we saw her. She was such a good baby. She fit into a family that was very busy with children involved in many activities.

Shortly after Shelbi was born, I had a roller-skating accident at cheerleading camp. That fall resulted in a broken elbow, which required surgery and several months of therapy. Ashley and Kari were great caretakers, not just for me, but especially for Shelbi. This was the beginning of her life with three moms!

I went back to my position as elementary principal in the fall of 1996. Shelbi stayed with a wonderful woman who also kept a little girl only four months older than Shelbi. Watching the two girls together was my first inclination that something was wrong. The other child began crawling; Shelbi never did. The other child started walking; Shelbi took her time. As she began to take steps, she fell often. The falls often resulted in a full fall, meaning she would not break the fall with her hands. She suffered a few nosebleeds and several bruises on her forehead.

This story begins right here, at the moment when I began to face the reality that something odd was going on. These were not just clumsy moments. These were real falls caused from something we could not understand or explain. I started seeking medical help through her primary physician. He sent us to a therapist who worked with Shelbi to teach her how to catch herself. This was an arduous task. For some reason, she did not seem to know she was falling. It was as if she could not tell anything different was happening. As I sat there watching all this, I knew I had some work to do.

I had to find out what was causing this condition. I had to know how to best meet my child's needs. I had to know how to not fall apart with whatever news I would find. I wanted to learn how to handle this, how to help, and how to be the mom Shelbi needed. How do you teach a two-year-old to know she is about to fall, or that something is falling out of her hands? I was so unprepared. Raising Ashley and Kari had been so different. They seemed to fit in the "norm" of growing stages. *How do I fix Shelbi? Why is this happening?* I needed answers.

Shelbi went through many months of learning to put her hands out when she fell. This worked while the therapist *caused* her falls; it did not work when the falls were *unexpected*. My eyes were opened to many new observations. I noticed how much we do daily that we never have to think about. For instance, we breathe, blink, and swallow without ever thinking about it. Shelbi had to think about many choices we never have to make. Her little smile never waned as she did just what she was told. The therapist tried to help her feel, sense, or observe the change of a fall, but this was almost impossible.

I would have to find a way to prevent falls. Surely, I could protect her. I knew this was foolish, even as I promised her I would protect her. Falls are a natural phenomenon. While she was learning to catch herself, we also discovered she was not swallowing well. Her pillowcase would be covered in saliva each morning. I began to put her hair up in a scrunchie at night to keep it out of her face. I noticed it for a while, but I did not think much of it, until she started coughing and kind of choking each morning. This clearing of her throat would last a good thirty minutes to an hour after she woke up.

We were introduced to a miraculous pediatric neurologist soon after more symptoms began to appear. He ordered a swallow test that revealed what we already knew. Now she would need to be made aware of what it feels like to swallow constantly, not just when she eats or drinks. We were shocked and dismayed, but not defeated. Once again, questions reeled through my head. *How do I explain this one?* The doctor also ordered an MRI (magnetic resonance imaging), which revealed brain damage in her cerebellum. The results of this test led the doctor to diagnose her with cerebral palsy.

I had heard about this but had never seen it up close. I began to research and ask lots of questions. But Shelbi's symptoms did not match up. She was not displaying the symptoms related to this diagnosis. The next three years were spent seeing eye doctors, having medical tests, and having doctors ask me what I wanted them to find. They did not see what I saw. They were not her mom. I would tell them I did not want to find anything wrong with Shelbi, but I did want to know I was doing everything I could to help her. *What am I missing? Where do I go for these answers?* Did you notice all the I's I just used? I was so sure I could figure this out. I did not include many, if any, others. My world became much smaller, and my focus was on one beautiful child who was struggling to walk, swallow, and see the world around her.

Shelbi was being tested, prodded, and amazed at by her physicians. Dr. Crisp called her "the irrepressible Shelbi." She has definitely lived up to that name. Before her first birthday, she was hospitalized with pneumonia and dehydration. She had swallow tests, gait discussions, eye exams, and many other doctor visits. She had exploratory surgery on her eyes. She had a tonsillectomy and wore braces to help move her teeth in alignment with her nose.

Swallowing did not come naturally. Choking was a very real danger. Shelbi learned to swallow in her own way. After about five years, the nighttime excessive salivating ceased. Sinus infections were treated several times a year and continue to plague her.

After a few years, Dr. Crisp ordered a follow-up MRI. It showed an increase in brain damage, which meant it could not be cerebral palsy. We were sent to a specialist in Houston at the children's hospital. That doctor checked her out and said he was pretty sure he knew what it was but sent us back to get genetic testing. Shelbi was tested and diagnosed with SCA8 (spinocerebellar ataxia type eight). We were given the following definition: An inherited neurodegenerative condition characterized by slowly progressive ataxia (problems with movement, balance, and coordination). This condition typically occurs in adulthood and usually progresses over decades. Common initial symptoms include dysarthria, slow speech, and trouble walking. Some affected individuals experience nystagmus and other abnormal eye movements. Life span is typically not shortened. This condition is inherited in an autosomal dominant manner, although not all individuals with abnormalities in the disease-causing gene will develop the disease.

Shelbi has an inherited disease. If that is the case, then her dad or I must have it also. Genetic testing revealed Ronald also has SCA8.

SCA8. This word describes the beginning and end of everything that follows. Shelbi never changed, but we did. We—her dad and I—had to rely on God to see us through not only the diagnosis but the days and years that were to follow. As we began researching, we found a convention taking place in San Diego. We flew out to learn more about SCA8 and how to face life with this in front of us. As we entered the convention's doors, we found a vast amount of people in wheelchairs. People of all ages. Many of them had service animals. Very few of the affected participants were walking around. My heart sank with this realization. As I think back now, I may have noticed more wheelchairs because that was my fear. Ronald and I talked to many attendees and presenters. We didn't find anyone with SCA8.

What did this mean? What were we facing? Our thoughts went wild with possibilities.

Shelbi will be in a wheelchair one day. She will need our help and attention for the rest of her life in a way that we could not even fathom at the time. She will lose the ability to swallow. She will not be able to communicate verbally. She will never run and play sports. How do we prepare for that? After more and more discussions, we realized that all types of ataxia were present in the participants. We were on our own. We were going to have to find out how to support Shelbi best through trial and error.

I do not know where to begin or how to express what I felt. Fear, denial, shock, anxiety, sadness, loneliness, and relief, in a way. Relief, only because I finally knew what was wrong. In 2001, Shelbi was among very few children who had this diagnosis, and she seemed to be the only one we could find who was walking and talking. God showed His divine love as her great physician. There is no cure. Medications are not available to stop the cells from atrophying. We can now begin to heal and live. Not heal in the sense that SCA8 will go away, but in the reality that we face the facts and get on with life. We will not need to continue to see doctors since there is no cure or medication that will help.

Shelbi's grandma, Ronald's mom, died a couple of weeks before we received the results of the genetic testing. He and I are certain she had SCA8. We do not know for sure without her being tested, but her symptoms matched all we had been studying. I cannot remember the exact dates when we began to see a change. Grandma showed symptoms for about three years before she passed away. It started with her losing her balance. We would go in her house to find her leaning over to one side as she sat on the couch. She fell a few times after that. One of the falls happened while she was standing in the bathroom and brushing her teeth. Another fall occurred when she was bending over to tie her shoes. I am certain she had other falls that we were unaware of. She went in the hospital for a while and quit walking altogether. Swallowing became a big problem for

Grandma. She would cough and choke at times. I am not aware if her eyes became worse or not. The doctors treated her for Parkinson's because some of the symptoms are the same. We never heard if any of her brothers or sisters had these symptoms. Her dad also lost his balance and had trouble with swallowing. We will never know if they had SCA8. I wish we had tried harder to contact family members. We could have asked them if these symptoms occurred in other relatives.

In the meantime, other children Shelbi's age were running up and down the bleachers with ease. I took her to every ball game, track meet, and one-act play her sisters were a part of. Shelbi did not climb, run, or move like them. She held her head to the side and squinted her eyes as she tried to focus on new situations. She could not lie down and watch television, but sat straight up and held her head sideways. Her eyesight was good, so far as we could tell. She played with Barbie dolls and all the small parts that go along with them. She colored pictures, and she learned her alphabet and many sight words. Her desire to learn and flourish was apparent as she took in the world around her.

She was able to swim at a very young age. Her babysitter said she swam like a fish. We realized that, in the water, Shelbi must feel totally in control of her body. She was able to take dance at age three and perform in a recital. We prayed that she would not fall off the stage. God held her up! She sang solos at church, memorized scripture, and loved everyone.

God never left our side. Right before Shelbi's first Thanksgiving, her sister was in a major four-wheeler accident. Kari was riding with a friend in our backyard when the gear stuck while they were ascending a small mound of dirt. The four-wheeler rolled back on top of the girls, and the gearbox hit right in the middle of Kari's face. She had to have extensive reconstructive face surgery. Many of you may know the feeling of helplessness when your child is in the hospital or sick, and there is nothing you can do. Shelbi stayed with her Grandma Charlene, while Ronald and I attended to Kari.

Shelbi was only nine months old. We knew she was in good hands, and God showed up as the great physician in my middle daughter's life. Kari recovered quickly and without any pain.

The life of Shelbi cannot be told without sharing what was happening around her, as well as what was happening within her. She is who she is because of her lived experiences.

At this stage of her life, God became the great physician (Matthew 9:12, NLT) to Shelbi and her family. We knew He would see her through and care for her in ways only He can. At night, when I was alone and away from Shelbi, I would cry and pray for complete healing. I felt hopeless at times and wanted, more than anything else, for her to be happy and whole. When I was with Shelbi, I put on a happy face. I never wanted her to see me sad about this. God comforted me in ways that are hard to describe but very real. I began to feel a peace that passed all understanding. Shelbi will be OK. She will be Shelbi, just like she is!

Kari, Shelbi, and Ashley (first Easter)

Dance recital

2

PROTECTOR

He will cover you with his feathers,
and under his wings you will find refuge.
His faithfulness will be your shield and rampart.

—PSALM 91:4 (NIV)

The elementary years proved to be a revelation of knowledge about this disease. I tried to find other parents of children with SCA8 to talk to. I found one, but their child was not talking or walking at the age of three. Shelbi was abounding with life. She walked, ran (sort of), talked, and talked, and talked. Many of the staff members at her school were very caring and showed compassion as they experimented with the best ways to meet her needs. Classroom work was not a problem, other than math. I was bound and determined that she learn to tell time and count money. We worked diligently at home to conquer the goals I set for Shelbi. I never bought her a digital watch or Velcro shoes. I felt these would hinder her from learning all she needed to learn. This was just the beginning of my fight and daily struggle in making sure Shelbi was "normal" and able to do all her sisters were able to do. Throughout the rest of this book, you will see that the Lord reminded me often of who He wanted Shelbi to be. He would use this disease to make her who she is today.

Shelbi's elementary years began without the diagnosis. The teachers Shelbi had from pre-K to second grade were amazing. They made it work. Shelbi was well taken care of. She was loved and worked with to be just as productive as the other students. They had to find ways to help her cut, write, color, read, and not trip over anything. She often dropped or spilled things, and she tripped over anything on the floor. Some teachers patiently helped her through the mishaps. Some teachers had a harder time showing that compassion. She often felt as if they were mad at her. I knew that was not true. Perceptions are real to the perceiver, and Shelbi continued this thought about the way people treated her. If any negativity or frustration was shown, she felt as if the person did not like her because she was different. These instances are not unique to people with disabilities, and they proved to be great lessons to both Shelbi and me. Throughout her lifetime, we learned together to accept negativity. I spent many hours explaining the reactions she encountered. Encouraging my young, precious little girl to keep smiling, keep trusting, and keep finding the best in people is a never-ending task. I want to explode or cry or complain but try not to.

Shelbi needed to understand she would face difficulties. During her third-grade year, I attended my first ARD (admission, review, and dismissal) meeting as a parent. An ARD is a meeting among teachers, therapists, diagnosticians, administrators, and parents or guardians. The purpose of the meeting is to discuss the disability and find ways to ensure success in the public-school setting. This was a mile marker for me. She had been diagnosed three years earlier. I never thought she would need special education. I had been present in many other ARDs during my years of teaching. Now I was on the other side of the table. This was very sobering. It did not take long to realize the depth of the pain and frustration parents faced upon noticing the difference that was obvious between their child and all the rest. This is a very real feeling. During this time, our definition of normal changed tremendously. The teacher Shelbi had in third grade was the first one who officially faced the job of making the legal accommodations and modifications work. She made Shelbi feel like a million bucks. Shelbi never acted like she noticed her difficulties. Normal to us looked more like this: Slower, meticulous hours of writing. Math lessons and homework that took us late into the night. Falls that were frequent and sometimes more painful than others. Peers who stepped up and helped her in so many ways. One story that I remember vividly is the day the school had a basketball-type race. Shelbi always wanted to be involved in anything that was going on. I made sure she knew she could do anything. Our Protector was with her as she and I figured out ways to make it work. Many times, God provided angels to aid our endeavors. This was one of those times. There was a young man who was a very good basketball player. He was in the lead and was set to win the race. Then he noticed Shelbi struggling. She would bounce the ball, lose the ball, bounce the ball, lose the ball. He stopped what he was doing and walked alongside Shelbi as she struggled to finish the race. Tears come to my eyes, even now, as I remember the true compassion of a young man who gave up winning to help my baby girl.

God's protection was shown in various ways throughout her elementary years. Her physical education teacher was a great help. He made sure to include her in all he could. Being in a very small school district, the facilities were not always conducive for people with disabilities. I wish I had known then what I know now. I had no idea that Shelbi was missing out on having more opportunities that would have truly benefited her. The school purchased her a special swing that had a back on it. When she reached the last years of elementary school, we found that she needed some further modifications. They had the steps that led to the cafeteria painted different colors, to let Shelbi know a step was there. Special handrails were added to a stall in the restroom to help her keep her balance. Each of these changes that were needed to help Shelbi sank deep into my heart. I kept wanting her to get better. Even in knowing there would be no cure, I kept wishing for improvement.

In other areas of her life, people provided love and support. One year, the community where our church was located held a Fourth of July parade. All the kids were going to decorate their bicycles and ride in the parade. A good friend of ours found out Shelbi could not ride a bike, with or without training wheels. He asked us if Shelbi might be able to ride a sturdy, three-wheeled bike. She thought so, and before she knew it, she had a bike for the parade. They built it, painted it with paint provided from a professional race car driver, and presented it to her in time to ride in the parade. This bike provided a way for Shelbi to fit in and not look out of place. She is twenty-six now. Her dad raised the seat and handlebars so she can still ride it. This is another example of the angels God provided along the way. If you are reading this, thank you for all the time you took to create this bike.

She also benefited from horseback riding. Her aunt helped her ride and taught her how to handle a horse. Shelbi also rode with a therapy group. On the back of a horse, she felt totally in control. Shelbi did not have to worry about walking straight, focusing so intently on the road ahead. She was able to just enjoy moving along on the back of a very stable horse. I loved watching this and I would cry, with grateful tears, as I realized how relaxed she looked.

Her sisters were in high school and involved in many extracurricular activities. These included cheerleading, volleyball, basketball, track, softball, and one-act plays. Shelbi and I never missed an activity. She was with us during each long drive and late-night event. Shelbi was, and is, an excellent traveler. She never griped or complained. We learned to sit lower in the stadium seats, but she still experienced many falls. It never slowed her down. She picked herself up, dusted off, and started over.

I watched as Shelbi began to maneuver between the regular classroom and therapy sessions that took place at school. Speech therapists, OTs (occupational therapists), and PTs (physical therapists) became very important in the life of Shelbi. They stayed involved to keep her moving. It was not a situation where they could set goals and then she would graduate out of therapy. She would need it to take place consistently throughout her public-school years and beyond. Many of her teachers played important roles in building her confidence as a strong young girl growing up with the difficulties she was experiencing. I remember many times watching her head into the school and praying for her to stay steady and safe. My heart was so heavy, not with fear, but with wondering what might happen next. My baby girl had to learn to watch for backpacks on the floor, kids running and pushing in line, and carrying a lunch tray by herself, all while focusing the best she knew how.

Ashley and Kari never treated her like anything was wrong. I do not remember asking them what they thought or how they felt. I know we talked about it, and I do remember Kari not acknowledging the disease at all. They included her in so many areas of their personal lives. I am so thankful that they never thought she was different. They were able to accept all she was and go with that. Both were so loving, kind, and patient with Shelbi. In fact, Ashley took Shelbi with her on her dates. (I thought that was a very smart move on my part) They taught her the lyrics to many songs, some of which I was surprised about. I found this out one Sunday night when we were headed to Gause Baptist Church for song night. Shelbi loved to sing in front of anyone. She announced that she was going to sing, "She Thinks My Tractor's Sexy"! I almost croaked. She did not sing that at church! I realized that night that the children's songs I taught Kari and Ashley were not what Shelbi was learning. She went right on to the teenage songs that her sisters were listening to.

Shelbi's Thoughts on the Elementary Years

"I remember the swing with the back on it. I remember when my best friend fell out of a swing and left in an ambulance. I was so scared that I would never see her again. I loved being in elementary school. Learning to read was very special to me. I loved books. One of the highlights was being able to attend the Burleson-Milam Special Olympics each spring. The workers did a fantastic job of helping each participant feel very important and super athletic! I still love to see some of my elementary teachers. They never treated me like I had a disability. Looking back at it now makes me appreciate them more and more."

At this time in Shelbi's life, God showed up as her Protector (Psalm 121, NLT). This name for God became more real as I watched His divine protection over my daughter's life. She felt it, and I observed it. Shelbi still fell, got discouraged, and faced ridicule and cruelness from classmates. She was also loved and cared for by most of them. I still struggle with dwelling on the bad. I want Shelbi to remember the good. She knew she was different but had no idea why. The tears at night became less as I began to accept the disease and determined to not let it define her. She will be all she can be. With the help of God, I will make sure of that.

Elementary school

Friend from ambulance story

3

SHEPHERD

Jesus said, "Let the little children come to me, and do not hinder them, for the kingdom of heaven belongs to such as these."

—MATTHEW 19:14 (NIV)

Shelbi's young life was filled with awe and excitement. I watched as God provided a way in every situation. She began talking about Jesus and who He was at a very, very young age. We talked to our pastor about this. At what age would we know that she really knew who Jesus was and what He had done for her? He said to ask her. So, when she was five years old, the pastor and I asked her. Did Shelbi know who Jesus was? Did she know what sin was? Did she know that Jesus died for her on a cross to save her from sin? Did she know He rose from that death and wants her to live with Him eternally? Her answers were not just yes to knowing all this, but a lengthy explanation for the reason she believed this. Right then, she prayed and asked God to be her Lord and Savior for the rest of her life. My dad was given the opportunity to baptize her soon after. Shelbi has never wavered from this decision. She has matured and developed different explanations now that she has experienced more of life, but she has never let go of that childlike faith that God will do what He says He will do. She was, and continues to be, a great inspiration to me and many others.

I was called to missions as an eighteen-year-old at a Billy Graham crusade in Houston, Texas. I always imagined going to Africa, or some faraway country, to work and live with another culture, but God had different plans for my missionary journey. After all, we are all called to share right where we are. I was asked to teach at a vacation Bible school on an Indian reservation near Ruidoso, New Mexico. Shelbi was six years old, and the organization that invited me did not allow children to go on mission trips. I asked for an exception, and they quickly agreed. It turned out she was a far greater blessing than any of us had expected. The Indians, the staff, and other volunteers from our group felt her amazing childlike love and saw her pure faith. The light of Christ was so apparent that others shared many stories with me. One time, she asked me if she could go up to the altar to pray. I was hesitant and felt like I should keep her out of the way since she was the only child from our group, but I let her go. After the service, a pastor told me that, as soon as she knelt, he felt God moving and watched as others began to follow her. She told me she was praying for some friends of hers who didn't know Christ as their Savior. I never hesitated after that to let her go forward when she felt led.

The Bible school class we taught on the reservation consisted of many children from the area who were about the same age as Shelbi. She helped me sing songs and play games that let them know about Jesus and His love for each of them. One little boy still sticks out in my mind who continually said there was no way Jesus could love him. Shelbi talked to him over and over. He kept coming to class, and he brought his family to the evening services. We went back for several years after that first summer and saw him each time. Shelbi and I do not know if he ever accepted the unconditional love that Jesus offers, but we still pray often for that precious young man.

Shelbi was prayed for, loved, and doted on at each mission trip she attended. I cannot name each one, but if you are reading this and remember us, thank you for being part of the "village" that helped raise my baby girl. Even apart from the trips, God sent people to change our lives.

One special lady loved Shelbi from the first time they met. She was so interested in her life and loved to sit and listen to Shelbi talk on and on. She found out about Shelbi's love for swimming, and that we lived in a small town without public access to a pool. This amazing lady paid for swimming lessons for Shelbi and shared many meals at Dairy Barn. I am so grateful for the love and care she showered on Shelbi and continues to even now.

These trips to New Mexico were a very influential part of her life. She taught Bible school classes, helped set up and take down decorations, and loved on all the little children brought our way. Some lifelong friendships were gained for Shelbi during these short ten days each summer. Her co-teacher during those trips is one of her best friends. She kept an eye out for Shelbi. I loved watching them laugh, teach, explore and enjoy sharing Christ with each of the children that attended Bible School.

Kari, Shelbi's sister, moved out of our home to go to college right after Shelbi turned seven years old. Our household changed again as we adjusted to life with just us. I found out that having only one child at home is completely different than raising two who are very close in age. Shelbi did not have anyone to compete with. We watched what she wanted to watch on television. We ate what she wanted to eat. Our world pretty much rotated around Shelbi and giving her the best life possible.

Shelbi continued to share with and pray for her friends. She regularly went to the altar to pray and cry that their hearts would allow Jesus in. For three years, she never gave up on the fact that they would know Him. Finally, at summer camp, she watched as, one by one, all three of them accepted Christ. God has been and is ever present in all Shelbi does. Her friends in elementary school were amazing. She was protected and cared for by many who saw her struggle. One special girl even pinned another classmate to the fence for making fun of Shelbi! Thank you! If you are reading this, I want you to know how much your kindness meant to us. God sent all kinds of angels to Shelbi's rescue.

Playing T-Ball at the age of five became another example of her determination. She played on a team made up of boys and girls. She loved it. Since she couldn't really explain what she was seeing or doing, I am going to share with you what I saw and felt each time she batted. Walk carefully to the batter's box. Please do not fall. Help umpire set up tee to right height and ask him to place ball on tee. Look out at team in the outfield, turn head slightly to the left to focus. Look down at ball on tee, focus on ball. Lift bat up to shoulder, focus on outfield one more time. Look at ball on tee, hold head straight down to see ball. Swing bat, connect! Put bat down and run as straight as possible to first base. Please don't let her fall. Then same thoughts as she ran from base to base. Please see the base. Run straight; don't trip. She loved playing T-ball. I could see her precious smile as she stopped on each base. I did make sure they put her far enough in the outfield to not encounter a ball moving in the air toward her. Her teammates cheered her on. She was able to play one year of T-ball, just like her sisters! On a side note, I remember once when she accidentally threw a bat at the umpire's shins. He was very gracious in his pain.

In addition to school and recreation, Shelbi was blessed with special opportunities to travel. Her oldest sister, Ashley, attended the American Musical and Dramatic Academy in Manhattan, New York. On Shelbi's seventh birthday, we took her to see her sister. This was a wonderful experience. It was about five degrees outside, and she got recognized on the *TODAY Show*. The most memorable part of the trip was her hair catching fire. We were all in Ashley's tiny apartment, singing "Happy Birthday"! Our attention was focused on singing and taking pictures, when she bent over to blow out the candles, and her pigtail fell into the flame. It was quickly extinguished, and no one was harmed!

I have one other quick story about New York. During one of our visits, we rented a car and drove to Niagara Falls. As we were going through the checkpoint to drive to the Canadian side, one of the guards leaned in and asked Shelbi if her dad knew she was leaving the country with her mom. She said, "No, I don't think he knows where I am"! I had to do a little explaining. Whew! We made it back safely.

We were involved in many mission trips, including the Indian reservation in New Mexico, a racetrack in Ruidoso, and the island of San Andrés, Colombia. Each of these trips was filled with adventure, pain, love, and special relationship building with others. Reaching others for Christ is very important to Shelbi, and people are automatically drawn to her. These trips included teaching Bible school, visiting women in prison, walking the streets of foreign countries, and meeting people who have the same love for Christ. God walked beside Shelbi and kept her upright. He gave her courage to speak about Him and to show love to others.

Shelbi's View
"I loved going on mission trips. One of my best friendships was formed at the racetracks of Ruidoso, New Mexico. The children were all precious. It was a privilege to get to teach and play with each of them. I am so glad my friends received Christ as their Savior. My relationship with Christ is number one in my life, and I want all my friends to know Him, too. Mom and I traveled a lot. She made sure I tried everything I wanted to, and some things I did not. I was always scared of climbing mountains because of my balance. Mom would push me to go ahead and give it a try. I was so glad after I made it up the mountain, even though many times on the journey up, I whined to my mom. I am glad now that she took me with her on all those trips."

My Shepherd became the name for God as He began to reveal Himself as her shepherd. He was showing her how to trust Him no matter what. The years that followed were going to test this trust. As I look back now, I realize each lesson learned in her early years was preparing us for the next chapter. If I had to do it all over, I would have paid more attention and enjoyed the blessings we received. The doctors told us this was a slow, progressive disease. She would most likely be using a walker and would then need a wheelchair in the next ten or so years. I knew that time was crucial. I did not want Shelbi to miss out on doing everything she possibly could while she was still walking.

Vacation Bible school at Ruidoso Downs in New Mexico

Missions

4

JOY

❧※❧

Do not grieve, for the joy of the Lord is your strength.

—NEHEMIAH 8:10 (NIV)

Writing about Shelbi's life is both rewarding and painful. The title of this chapter is "Joy." That is almost an oxymoron. As I look back at her junior-high years, I remember many more tears and struggles than joyful moments. The joyful part came in Shelbi herself. She was, and is, a joy to be with. She had the ability to find good when I wanted to lay down and cry. Her strength allowed us both to experience the joy of the Lord.

Junior high school brought about a new set of difficulties and miraculous strengths. Her classmates, who had been ever present in elementary school, became active in sports and engaged in activities that Shelbi could not participate in. I got the privilege to be her sixth-grade teacher. This brought on a whole new set of problems. I wish I had done some things differently, but I was proud of how Shelbi handled it. One of my biggest mistakes was what I taught one day in science. We were studying DNA and what it all means.

I shared Shelbi's prognosis with the class, which included the word *disease*. From that day forward, many of those classmates stayed clear. They didn't want to catch SCA8. When new people moved in, some of her friends would undoubtedly fill them in on the girl with the disease. They missed the part of the lesson that showed it was not contagious. She had some friends stick by her side, no matter what she could or could not do. Some friends moved on. This was tough, as it is on most junior-high students. It is hard to begin to look forward to high school and, at the same time, look back and enjoy childhood.

Both of Shelbi's sisters were cheerleaders, and she wanted to follow in their footsteps. I had small uniforms made for her from the time she could walk. She would dance and move her arms while cheering and smiling. I did not think it would be a good idea to let her try out for cheerleading. As her mom, I knew she would have trouble getting out of the way if a player ran toward the sidelines. I also knew that learning the cheers, chants, and dances would be extremely difficult for Shelbi. Her ability to move was fine, but it was not as quick as others. I had been a high school cheerleader sponsor for almost fifteen years. I knew what I wanted in a cheerleader, and I knew Shelbi would struggle. Then God showed up, as He always did. He never left. I spent a lot of time trying to fix her situations and make her happy in my own strength. I was never able to do it without His complete help.

Needless to say, I let her try out for junior-high cheerleader, and she was elected. She loved cheering and enjoyed being a part of the cheer team. It was as hard as I thought it would be. I worked and worked with her to increase her speed and ability to move without falling. Her sponsor was great and made sure she was always safe. Watching Shelbi cheer was both heart-wrenching and elating. She smiled, laughed, moved her arms and legs as best she could, and enjoyed it all. I saw her struggle to move fast enough to not look odd, to stay in the back during dances, and to not show missed steps. My heart would stand still as I smiled and cheered her on. I was so proud of her determination during each of her difficulties. In eighth grade, the one-act play became another place of safety and pride. Her teachers loved her, watched out for her, and included her in everything they could. Watching her on stage brought on the same emotions as cheerleading. The volleyball coach asked her to be the manager in eighth grade, and she kept that position throughout high school. This allowed Shelbi to be around the athletes, travel to the games, and feel very important. My other daughters were in all those activities, and I began to realize how differently I felt with Shelbi's involvement. I wanted to take her home, surround her with pillows, and hold on as tightly as I could. That's not living. I knew she had to try it all and learn with each step. Shelbi attended dances and did her best to never sit down during one. She still loves to dance and listen to music. I do not remember much more that happened in sixth, seventh, and eighth grades that really stands out. Most days brought about new obstacles we had not even thought about.

One of those obstacles happened in junior high when she was asked if she wanted to attend her ARD. This is the process schools use to help students with disabilities navigate through public school. Shelbi's first ARD meeting was planned to be sure her teachers knew about her balance issues, and to make sure the physical education teacher knew her limitations. It also provided for a physical, occupational, and speech therapist to work with Shelbi on a regular basis. With each passing year, we were able to get Shelbi the help she needed to be successful. She was not sure about going to her ARD, but I assured her she would find it interesting. As I look back at Shelbi's first exposure to this, I wish I had prepared her more. I found out very quickly that Shelbi was not as keenly aware of how many problems she had. My efforts to never deny her access to new opportunities, and to push her to be all she could be, hid the fact that anything was wrong. She listened in on that first ARD, stared at me, cried, and kept silent; that is, until we got home. The questions came pouring out as I explained SCA8 and all the implications that are attached to it. I told her we did not have anyone or any resource that could tell us exactly what to do to fix it. We were to live each day to the fullest and be thankful for what we could do. At one of these ARDs, Shelbi met a man who would change the trajectory of her life. He was assigned as her transition counselor. This man's name was Mr. Wright, and he was definitely our "Mr. Right"! He saw in Shelbi what I saw. She would go far, and nothing was going to stop her. As that part of her plan was developing, my heart, once again, was breaking. She explained to the ARD committee about her difficulties in class. She had to focus and wait for her eyes to get still when she looked at the board. Then, if she had to take notes or work a problem, she had to refocus and wait for her eyes to get still. This refocusing was constant and was beginning to cause her to get behind and miss concepts, and it kept her from listening while she was focusing. They added note-taking assistance to her accommodations along with a few other changes. Hearing the words out loud made it real. I could no longer deny the help she would need to succeed educationally. She was visibly tired after school. It was not the kind of tired where you could take a nap and feel rested. The doctor explained it to me like this: Shelbi's eyes are unbalanced due to the ataxia. She looks at the board and must work to hold her eyes steady to read what she needs to read. She looks down at her paper and must do the same to write the assignment. She does this over and over, which puts stress on her brain. This wears her out. This was hard to explain to each teacher and became more difficult in her final years of public school. I am sure, somewhere deep inside, I knew this day would come. I was hoping it could wait.

Shelbi's Thoughts on the Junior-High Years

I loved cheering, and yet, this was when I began to realize how different I was. I remember teachers who were very helpful. I had fun with my friends. Our sixth-grade field trip to Galveston is still a great memory. My mom loved taking her students to Moody Gardens and sharing her love for Galveston with them.

God is truly the one who brings joy. Shelbi and I found joy in the midst of all the changes. As the road of life became more difficult to maneuver, God led us on His path. He always wants us to live life to our full potential. Her limitations were real, but God gave her amazing strength and joy.

Junior-high cheerleader

5

ROCK/COMFORTER

The Lord is my Rock, my Fortress and my Deliverer.
My God is my Rock, in whom I take refuge, my shield
and the horn of my salvation, my stronghold.

—PSALM 18:2 (NIV)

I have told you these things, so that in me you may
have peace. In this world you will have trouble.
But take heart! I have overcome the world.

—JOHN 16:33 (NIV)

High school brought on a whole new set of obstacles. This chapter has two verses that held us during the four years. The title of this book was developed from what happened during Shelbi's teenage years. The people who were insistent on telling her no, or that she could not, made her stronger and were very beneficial in building the determination and confidence she has today. Shelbi's final public-school years were filled with adventure.

She had many good times. I wish I could only write about those. It is through adversity that all of us grow, and this is where I want you to realize how you can take the negative and turn it around for good. To see the hardship she experienced is crucial to see how she overcame. Some teachers were compassionate and caring, while others seemed determined to make Shelbi's life miserable. I know that sounds harsh, but the stories contained in this chapter are all true. I don't say lightly that Shelbi was a joy. She truly enjoyed life. She was easy to teach and even easier to love. Those who realized this were successful in bringing out the best in Shelbi. She was coming into her own, just like all teenagers, and she faced each day with much self-determination. It was not that I did not want her to be seen like all the other students, but I knew she was different and had her own identity. I can see now how those with disabilities struggle to be who they are and try to fit into the world of everyone else around them. It's difficult for me to say that not all educators are compassionate, or even kind, at times. I was in public education for thirty-two years as a teacher and principal. I believe I was guilty of not meeting the needs of all students with special needs. As a teacher, I saw these students as struggling just to show up each day, and I did not want to add another burden. This caused me to not push them to their full potential. As a mom, I wanted Shelbi to learn everything she could. I wanted her to have to work to get her education. I never wanted anything to be handed to her just because it took her too long or because she wrote slowly and deliberately. The teachers I taught with varied greatly in how they approached the profession. I am sure many of you who are reading this found the same to be true. I bet you can remember your favorite teachers and your worst ones. This also breaks my heart. Many of the teachers who caused pain to Shelbi were my co-workers. I even thought we were friends. I am certain it was not intentional, but it hurt nonetheless. Being employed in the same district where Shelbi went to school kept me from advocating for her. I was unable to voice what I really felt about how she was being mistreated. This was totally my fault. I did not

THANKS FOR TELLING HER "NO"

want the confrontation. I will not name names or throw rocks, but I do want you to understand that Shelbi had to grow up fast. She had to experience adults being cruel and unfair. She experienced so-called friends and peers pulling useless pranks just to see her fall. Some kids would leave backpacks in her way just to watch her trip. Others would throw things and snicker when she was hit by them. Each incident was a lesson in life that strengthened Shelbi. She also had faithful friends. She had friends who carried her lunch tray, helped tie her shoes, put her hair in a ponytail, and encouraged her every day.

One particularly tough day occurred during gym class. Shelbi had accommodations put in place for extra time at the beginning and end of class. She was never counted tardy. Getting dressed and ready for PE (physical education) was quite a task. Due to her lack of fine motor skills, tying her shoes was very difficult. In fact, she could not tie them successfully. Her friends would help when they could. One day, though, they all had to hurry to not get in trouble themselves. The day I am remembering was her being late to PE class. Her teacher punished her by making her run timed horses. I think that was what it was called. She had to start at one end of the gym, run to a certain point, reach down and touch a line, then run back and repeat this all the way down the gym. With any balance issues, bending down is difficult, much less trying to do this while running. Ataxia affects that balance even more. Nevertheless, Shelbi did what she was told to do to the best of her ability. She came home and fell apart. She did not understand her punishment, much less why she was being punished. Her dad and I spoke with the administration about the incident, and Shelbi was moved to a different PE class. In that class she was safe and taken care of but was not getting the physical fitness she needed. I was thankful for the peace this coach brought to Shelbi, so I did not push for physical activity. I should have learned a very important lesson about speaking up for Shelbi and teaching her to do the same, but I was as afraid of conflict as Shelbi was. I seemed to always look for the best in people and believed they would not hurt my daughter on purpose. I instilled this same idea in Shelbi. I still don't think I should expect bad in people, but Shelbi and I have both learned to be more prepared for the possibility.

Shelbi and her friends soon turned sixteen. They got their driver's licenses, and Shelbi's doctors told her no (there's that word again). She would not drive. She had a very slow reaction reflex, double vision, and nystagmus, and she lacked fine motor skills. This was devastating to a sixteen-year-old young lady. I let her drive on our dirt roads, and she loved it. I decided to let her try it out on a paved road. We went to a farm market road near our house, and she drove wonderfully, until a car appeared in the rearview mirror. Shelbi began to panic, and she became so nervous that she never wanted to drive again. I knew better than to push her at this point, so she stopped driving. Dating was another issue. Remember the disease I mentioned in the last chapter? That was not easily forgotten. She attended homecoming dances, proms, and other social events, but she did not date much.

Shelbi's senior year was also a year of extreme trials for her and her family. This was the year of great upheaval for me as her mom. The joy I told you about was constantly being bombarded, and I was afraid at one point that she would not recover. In her high school, at the beginning of the students' senior year, they sign a contract about raising money, having good attendance, passing grades, and keeping good behavior to attend the senior trip. If you did not meet the expectations, you were not allowed to go on the trip. The contract was put into place to discourage senioritis! It helped the seniors stay in school, make good grades, and not cause too many problems. Shelbi had heard about this trip for years, and she could not wait. In September of her senior year, Ashley and her family were called to be missionaries in the Philippines. Her husband went ahead of the family to find housing for them. Ronald and I were going to help Ashley wrangle her kids over miles and miles of air travel. I checked with the administration and changed the dates of travel to when I was told it would work best. I was given permission to take Shelbi with us as we traveled to the Philippines to help get her sister's family moved in. She had not yet signed the contract for the senior trip. One of her teachers was really excited for her. She even asked her to make a PowerPoint about the trip and all that she was able to experience. She was gone from school for six days. When Shelbi returned to school, she signed the contract and began to enjoy football season of her senior year. She suffered some illness and missed some more days of school later in the semester. In January, she was told that she could not go on the senior trip. She was completely heartbroken. I explained that she had not signed the contract until after we had returned from the Philippines, she had doctors' notes for her absences, and the administration had approved the absences. They did not change their minds. Shelbi kept smiling and kept studying, but she was so sad. She cried and asked why, but I could not find an acceptable answer. I was just as heartbroken. I could not fix this problem, but I knew who would see us through. God never left her side. The blessings she encountered in the Philippines far outweighed a senior trip, but that does not lessen the pain for an eighteen-year-old young lady.

At this same time, Shelbi was fitted for prisms to try to help with her vision. They told us that correcting double vision could affect her nystagmus, and correcting the nystagmus could affect her double vision. The prisms affected everything. She was nauseous and off-balance (more than usual), and she could not find a focus point. She could not wear them very long. We went back to just her eyes.

Not all of high school was miserable. I hate that we allow bad things to stand out the most. She had a lot of fun, and God continued to keep her walking and talking. The one-act play teachers kept her involved in acting and protected her from falling off the stage. Several of her fellow actors also played a huge part in making her feel normal! She continued to manage the volleyball team. One of the greatest experiences she was able to accomplish was marching in the Macy's Thanksgiving Day parade with all the other cheerleaders.

Her sisters had performed in 1999 and 2001. She was able to watch them on television and always hoped she could attend. Each step of this opportunity showed us the miracles that still happen in all our lives. We knew the length of the parade, the early morning hours, the eight-hour practices, and the speed of the routine would all be a challenge. As the sponsor and I started working with the girls, we became more and more excited at how much Shelbi could keep up. She helped us tweak some moves for Shelbi, and we were heading to New York City (miracle number one). Upon arrival, we found out that, for the first time, the cheerleaders would start at Macy's for their performance, then ride the subway back up to become the end of the parade (miracle number two). Shelbi was able to attend the long practices and maintain a positive attitude, until Sunday night. She came to Sherry and I and said, "I can't do it." That was the first time I had ever heard her say that. She said the routine was too fast, not because she couldn't do the motions, but because they had to shift positions and practically run to get in new places. We told her to wait until the actual practice in front of Macy's. If she still wanted to quit, we would let her watch from the sidelines with us. On the night of that practice, we could barely see them. Sherry climbed up a pole to video Shelbi to see what the problem was so we could come up with a solution. Of course, God had already set that in motion. A wonderful girl from Alabama (I think) interfered with our plans. She talked to one of our cheerleaders after noticing Shelbi's struggle. Once she heard about her abilities, she asked Shelbi if she could hold her waist and go with her as she moved. She became God's hands and feet for Shelbi that day. Shelbi was so excited (miracle number three). The grueling practices continued and brought about other concerns for Shelbi. Any time she gets tired, each of her symptoms are exaggerated. She falls more, has trouble seeing, drops things, etc. They had to be up early, fully dressed for the parade, eat breakfast, and catch the subway to Thirty-Fourth Street. She woke up rested and fully equipped for the day (miracle number four). The rest of the day was a blur. They all performed wonderfully, I might add, rode the subway back to where the end of the parade was, and followed Santa's sleigh through the rest of the parade (miracle number five). God is so good. I thanked Alabama (that's what I named her, since I only knew where she was from). I told her how God used her to be His hands and feet, and that she was a miracle for us.

Shelbi attended her junior and senior proms. She loved getting all dressed up and going to a dance. Two of her best friends accompanied Shelbi and her date to her first prom. They did not actually attend the prom but were with Shelbi as she prepared. They helped her stay balanced as she took pictures and got in and out of the truck. As I have said many times, it takes a village. This was one of those times. The extra care from her friends made the day spectacular.

High school continued. She had to add more accommodations as her disease slowly progressed. She needed large print for the state tests. This led to her high school counselor telling her that she was not college material. The counselor told Shelbi she should pursue a career that did not require a college degree. She could not take dual-credit classes and had to finish her final two years of high school without taking any honors courses. This move led her to be placed in a class with different peers than she'd had for the first two years. She had friends in both classes but had drawn really close to those heading into taking college classes. I did not fight hard enough but told Shelbi she can do anything she puts her mind to. We would deal with college (or not) after high school. That was the *no* that Shelbi heard so loudly we decided it should be the title of this book. She set her mind, then and there, to prove the noes wrong. Because of this no, Shelbi has accomplished way more than she ever thought possible. So, I can truly say, "Thank you for telling her, no"! She was given a wonderful aide to sit in her math classes, take notes for her, and help her understand.

Sooner than I thought possible, Shelbi was approaching her graduation day. The miracle in that was that she was able to walk across the stage. I was given the blessing of presenting her diploma. This was such a privilege, and tears rolled down my eyes as I watched my beautiful, determined young daughter walk up the few stairs, across the stage, and down the few stairs without ever stumbling. This was a milestone in our lives, and we had no idea what would happen next.

Looking back at all this was painful for me. In fact, I put off writing this chapter for two years because I did not want to relive it. Parents understand just how hard it is to see their children hurt. Some pain they bring on themselves, and other pain is brought on them. Neither pain is easy to handle. I was one of those parents who held in all that I was feeling. I did not want Shelbi to know I was hurting also. I assured her that all would work out, and it did.

Shelbi's Thoughts on High School

"I loved being in one-act play. The directors were amazing. They made sure to include me in every way possible. Being the volleyball manager was also fun. The coach made me feel needed, although I knew I could not do nearly as much as she needed me to. I had some encouraging teachers, and some who hurt me. My circle of friends narrowed greatly to just a select few. I found myself being less outgoing. It was not that all my friends walked away, but I felt different and stayed at arm's length. It was a time in my life when I had very little self-esteem. I did not speak up for myself, and I kept quiet about many things that were bothering me. I was heartbroken about the senior trip. I wanted to parasail with my classmates! I had been looking forward to that throughout my high school years. I still do not understand why I could not go."

This was the hardest part of the book to write. Struggles, defeats, pain, and sorrow are always difficult areas to go back to and examine. I know that Shelbi would not be who she is today without each of the experiences she had in high school. They set in motion her ability to find the good and go forth. I am so thankful God was my rock during those four years. The need for that firm foundation was very strong. As the ground shook, and I felt like I would be swallowed up, God showed up and stood me on that very rock. He never left our sides.

Scuba diving in the Philippines

Macy's Thanksgiving Day parade

Prom with help of friends

High school graduation

6

WAYMAKER

*This is the message which we have heard from Him and declare
to you, that God is light and in Him is no darkness at all.*

—1 JOHN 1:5 (NKJV)

A new day, a new chapter! Shelbi graduated from high school. Now what? Being told no about taking dual-credit college courses caused doubt as to what the future would hold. The positive side of me told her she could do anything she wanted to do. The negative side told me to let her down easy or guide her in a way that success would be easy and certain. The negative approach never worked. She would do what she wanted. I knew it would not be easy, but I felt certain it could happen. Her transition counselor arranged a visit to Texas A&M University to observe a special program for adults with disabilities. Postsecondary Access and Training in Human Services, or PATHS, is a program that provides students a chance to attend Texas A&M for one year. Shelbi said no. She could not see how this program would benefit her. The second time we visited the class, she changed her mind. She wanted to go for it. She knew it would only result in a certification for a program offered at Texas A&M. If she could not be a "traditional" Aggie, this would be the next best thing.

This one-year certification program prepares students to work as direct support professionals (DSP). Individuals in these positions support people with disabilities and older people to ensure their ability to live independently in their homes, with their families, or in other community settings. During the year, these students are also taught professionalism, self-advocacy, and how to be as independent as possible within the range of their diagnosis. To make this happen, Shelbi would attend a four-week summer program. She would live in on-campus housing, have a roommate, and be considered an A&M student. This was how our new journey began.

In July 2014, less than two months since high school graduation, I attended Bridge to Career (a summer program to prepare for PATHS) orientation with Shelbi. We went through all the meet and greet times and set up her dorm room. Her roommate shared similar tastes in music and their love of people. Probably one of the hardest things I faced with Shelbi was leaving her alone for any amount of time. The directors told me I had to go. She did not even cry! I decided to hang out around the dorm for a little while. I watched, from across the street, as she and her newfound friends headed to the cafeteria. I made sure she was safely inside before I could bear to drive away.

As a mom of a child with a disability, or a mom of their youngest child, or a mom in general, my head said, *Let her go*, and my heart said, *Go back and get her*. Of course, Mom knows best! Wow! I had a lot to learn during those four weeks, and even more during the rest of the program. Yes, you read that right: I had a lot to learn! True independence can only happen when the person is allowed true independence. Now I had to give Shelbi a chance to be Shelbi without me. The main purpose of the program may have been to certify Shelbi with skills to be employable in the field of DSP, but this program changed the path of her life. She learned so much more than skills for work. She learned how to live life, free from the confines of her home. It was not easy, by any means. Many tears, both hers and mine, were shed throughout the year. She wanted to come home and try something else at times, but Shelbi was never one to quit. She stayed determined and engaged in completing the program. The friendships that were created are still important to her today. They bonded as a family and saw each other through.

Brazos Valley Center for Independent Living (BVCIL) played a big part in supporting this program. You can find a center for independent living in almost any large town. They provide support in various ways. Shelbi was taught to cook without burning herself, wash clothes, exercise, budget money, and manage time. These skills are essential in aiding her day-to-day living. As you can see, I may have spoiled her just a little. Her dad and I cooked for her, washed her clothes, cleaned her room, and gave her money when she needed it. She was also encouraged to get a driver's license. No way! I had to draw the line somewhere. Even if Shelbi could learn to drive on public roads, how could I possibly stop all the other traffic from interfering? Fortunately for me, the doctors agreed. The neurologist said to make sure the optometrist felt it was safe. and vice versa.

Another great achievement gained from PATHS was the courage to go to college and work toward a bachelor's degree. The first step was to apply for Blinn College. Most of you know that colleges require an entrance exam. What I didn't know was that you do not have to pass it to be accepted. You can be assigned to take extra remedial classes to assure your success in college courses. This was the case for Shelbi. She almost passed the English part but did not do well on the Math section. Shelbi began looking for nearby housing and excitedly awaited her graduation from PATHS.

During PATHS, Shelbi met another man who would change her life's path. He wrote the foreword you read at the beginning of this book. He wanted to mentor her to become a People Planning Together trainer. This training brings together individuals with intellectual and developmental disabilities (IDD) to learn how to develop a person-centered plan based on how the person chooses to live their life. He worked with Shelbi for a couple of years before she was named the first certified peer-to-peer trainer in Texas. What a wonderful honor and accomplishment! Shelbi has used this training experience to share her story with others. This gives her a chance to give back and encourage others to never give up.

At the conclusion of PATHS, Shelbi was given the honor of being awarded the Director's Award. This is one of the most prestigious awards given by the program. The Director's Award is an all-around award for an exemplary student who mirrors the Aggie code of honor and trust; a student who gives 100 percent every day, who provides peer support, and represents the program in the community well and with honor. This was very humbling to us. Shelbi loves all, cares about all, and wants everyone to do their best. Giving a speech at graduation came with this honor, and Shelbi stole our hearts. This was the moment when I knew she would be a motivational speaker. She was amazing! She talked to the audience like she was talking to her best friend. We laughed and cried, and I was bursting with pride. I was so proud of how she had stayed with it. I am so proud of how determined she is to keep going, and I'm especially proud of this young lady who perseveres.

On the top of her graduation cap, she wrote, "I'll Be Back," meaning that she would return to Texas A&M University as a full-time student. I believe, at this point, I began to wonder why I had told her she could do anything she wanted to do. I knew how tough it was to get accepted into A&M. How was I going to explain this, and convince her to go to another college? Once again, I cried tears of frustration and dismay. I wanted her to be an Aggie if she wanted to be an Aggie.

Shelbi's Thoughts on PATHS

"Scary. I was away from my family for the very first time. Texas A&M is huge, and I was not sure I could do it. I met great friends and had wonderful staff who helped me all along the way. This was how I learned to be independent. I was forced to keep going or quit, and I knew

I would not quit. I learned to accept things around me that did not go my way. I knew I would not become a DSP. I always wanted to be a teacher, and finding success in the program would help me. I discovered many abilities I possessed that I was not quite aware of. When I finally started living life fully on my own, I finally started living."

The newness of life outside of public school proved to be just what we needed. God became our waymaker as He opened door after door to let Shelbi grow. I needed this guidance as I began to let go. It is not easy to allow true independence to a child who has so heavily relied on you in the past. I learned quickly that Shelbi could do so much more than I had allowed. I had thought I was helping her out by doing so many things for her. After all, she had a disability and needed me. That was so wrong. She had, and has, all the tools she needed to be completely independent. I had been holding her back. God was making a *way*!

"I'll Be Back

First certified peer-to-peer trainer in Texas

7

PROMISE KEEPER/ OVERCOMER

*"For I know the plans I have for you," declares
the Lord, "plans to prosper you and not to harm
you, plans to give you hope and a future."*

—JEREMIAH 29:11 (NIV)

College! Do you remember what I told you Shelbi had been told *no* about? She had been told that college was not in her future. She would not be able to attend classes, study, and successfully earn a degree. Shelbi trusted in the one who said He had plans for her. Not in a school counselor, teacher, doctor, or friend, but in the one who makes promises and keeps them. I let her choose the verse for this chapter, and she chose well. This is one of her favorite verses. Each time she faces a new obstacle, and they come at her all the time, she remembers this promise. He has a plan. His plan is best, and it is to prosper her. We know that we do not always get answers to prayers in the way we would like them to be, but we always get answers. If the answer is to wait, we pray for patience to wait. If the answer is no, we plan another route. If the answer is yes, we know that He will see us through. I say all that to say this: Shelbi was about to attend college.

She was accepted at Blinn College. She found housing right next door so she could walk to the campus. Texas Workforce Commission was going to fund her college experience, which was a wonderful blessing. They have certain requirements in order for someone to receive this funding. One of these is that Shelbi had to be enrolled as a full-time student. In her case, that meant twelve credit hours. She and I were not sure if this would work. She gets tired easily due to the focusing and refocusing of her eyes each time she looks up, down, or side to side. I found out that her neurologist could write a note describing her disability, and she could take less hours. She took only six her first semester. We realized this part of her journey was going to take a long time.

As you have seen throughout my storytelling, God always shows up. This time, He showed up through the life of one very special professor. She encouraged Shelbi in every way, not just while she was in her class, but even all these years since. She helped me even more. I was so worried about my baby taking classes where I could not take notes, listen to directions, and learn alongside her. She was on her own and was quite capable of doing it all. This professor kept assuring me of what she saw in Shelbi. As a mom, I knew I had to let her try, and be there whether she failed or succeeded. I was still working full-time and was unable to be with Shelbi physically, so we called each evening and worked through the day's events.

Blinn was a huge struggle for Shelbi. She has the best memory I have seen and can repeat back to me everything she learns, but she cannot pass a written test. No matter how much time she is given or who reads it out loud, she is not a written test-taker. This fact was extremely discouraging every time she failed a test. She was a great student, otherwise. She was always on time, sat in the front of the room, asked for help, completed all homework early, and did every extra credit assignment that was available. No matter how good the grades were that she received for all that, she hated failing the tests. We prayed each time she left to take a test. We prayed that all that she had studied would come to her, and for her to not be nervous but confident in her knowledge. Those prayers were answered much differently than I wanted. She continued to fail, over and over. I had a very hard time trying to convince her that it was OK. I wanted her to know that test grades do not define you.

Miraculously, she passed the classes. Little by little, she had six hours, then nine more, then she took a full twelve hours during her third semester at Blinn. Shelbi passed each class, even though she seldom passed a test. A side note here for all of you who are taking college classes or are scared to: You can pass with hard work, perfect attendance, completing all assignments on time, and asking questions. You do not have to be a good test-taker. Shelbi would want me to tell you, "You can do it." God will see you through. Trust Him in all things.

Living on her own during most of these three years was also a huge miracle. She was able to heat things up in a microwave, cook grilled cheese sandwiches, and wash her own clothes. She learned to buy shoes that did not need tying, and we cut her hair short so that she could fix it on her own. Many messes were made, but she cleaned them up through tears and frustration and kept on going. One weekend, she was at home and asked me to pour her milk for the cereal she was about to eat. I loved to help her but asked who poured her milk at the apartment. She looked up at me and said, "I do, but I like the way you pour it better." I told you she was just a little spoiled.

She truly enjoyed many of her classes. History came alive through another wonderful professor. Last summer, we visited Monticello, which was one of the places he had described in detail. She loved it and remembered all she was taught.

Before long, Shelbi was edging closer and closer to receiving an associate's degree from Blinn. She still was determined to go to Texas A&M. With the help of a special family friend, Shelbi and I were encouraged to give it a try. She gave us the name of a wonderful adviser who explained all Shelbi would need to do to be ready to attend. I knew God was with us, but I was preparing a way in my head to explain to Shelbi why she wouldn't be accepted. Texas A&M University is one of the top-ranking universities in the nation. Whoop! I might be biased; I am a graduate of the class of 1984. Attending Texas A&M would be a dream come true. When Shelbi enrolled for the final classes she could take at Blinn, we knew it was time to apply. Then we waited.

Shelbi was able to take fifteen hours during her last semester at Blinn. I moved in with her in January 2018 when I became the program director for the PATHS program Shelbi had attended. We are great roommates. That is, if I clean up my messes and don't clutter the living room. Living with any roommate demands give and take. Even though we're a mother-daughter team, there was much to learn about living in an apartment together. Sharing a room, bathroom, and one closet taught us much about compromise. We managed to enjoy living in the same house, and still do. We value each other's space, and we truly enjoy our time with one another.

During this adjustment period of learning to live together, the letter arrived. In early March, she received her acceptance to Texas A&M! She got in! She had been accepted. She would be the Aggie she so wanted to be. My heart soared, and I wanted to kick myself for doubting. God is so good. He knew whose lives she would touch and sent her right into the thick of it. My baby girl, who struggled to get the GPA she needed for acceptance, had done it! She only passed two or three of the many tests she took at Blinn. The success at Blinn was due to her sincere dedication to college. She never missed a class. She sat at the front of the room to soak it all in. Shelbi completed every assignment, not only on time, but early. She also made sure to take advantage of every extra credit opportunity that was offered. She graduated in May of 2018 with an associate's degree from Blinn College.

Outside of college, she continued to explore new adventures. She started dating a wonderful young man who was involved with Special Olympics. This led Shelbi to start swimming again. At first, she just swam for fun and to get exercise. When this young man's parents realized she was a swimmer, they encouraged her to join the team. She loved swimming, but even it produced obstacles that she had not thought about. Being in the water made Shelbi feel safe and in control. Diving in the water was another story. Many Olympic swimmers dive in to give them a great start. Shelbi worked and worked at it. She swallowed lots of water, and she finally decided she would have to make her big start from in the water, pushing off the side. She went on to win several races in the Special Olympics.

Shelbi decided to pursue a degree in university studies, mainly because it kept her from having to take any more math courses. She majored in agricultural leadership and minored in communications and youth development. She loved all her classes at A&M. These were classes that finally had to do with what she loved. One of her first professors at A&M made sure she was taken care of. His class was in a room where the students entered at the top in the back and walked down a set of stairs to find their seats. Shelbi needed to be in the front row to record each lesson. He went out of his way to show her a back way to enter his class. She would come out at the front row with no fear of falling down the stairs. God provided many little gifts like this in the form of people who were kind and compassionate.

Other professors were also kind. During her last year at A&M, her communications teacher decided to give Shelbi the opportunity to talk out a test. She took the time to ask her the questions and let Shelbi talk about what she knew. Shelbi aced that test! Finally, someone had taken the time to see what Shelbi knew, not just whether she could put it on paper. This was a life changer for Shelbi. She became more confident and continued to push through. The next semester, she met with another professor who agreed to give it a try. This also led to passing his tests. I was able to sit in on her visit with the second professor, and I was impressed with the care he took to find out what would be best for her to be successful.

I lived with Shelbi in College Station during the week and went to Milano on the weekends. Her daddy understood what it meant for me to be with Shelbi all through this journey. I was her chauffeur, short-order cook, study partner, scribe, mom, and friend during her years at A&M. Our family was extremely supportive during this time. Most of my focus was on Shelbi. Allowing her true independence meant I needed to be with her. Not really! She could have done most of it on her own. Living with her allowed me the opportunity to watch it unfold.

Before I finish this chapter, I have one more miracle to share. Hold on tight! Shelbi was able to get her driver's license. The doctors finally agreed, at the same time, about letting her try. Getting her permit was easy. She loved learning all the information and passed the test easily. Driving was a different matter. We started practicing. First, we spent a lot of time in parking lots, on our dirt road, and down less traveled streets. She became more and more confident as we practiced. The time came for her driver's test. We went to the Austin Driving School in Bryan for that. This is an excellent place to go to get your license. The people are so nice and helpful. From the first moment, Shelbi felt at ease and ready to give this a try. I sent her off with the tester and started praying. I must confess that I was praying for her not to pass. It was not that I did not want her to drive, but I did not want her to drive! This is my baby girl. I want to protect her in every way. I realize that God wants to protect her even more than I do. While I was waiting, I told God that I wanted His will about her driving. She passed her test! She not only passed but passed with almost a perfect score. We were both so excited, but I must admit, I was a little scared. Shelbi would now, at the age of twenty-four, be able to drive. She would need a car. I wanted to buy her an army tank for more protection.

One of Shelbi's special memories of A&M was her opportunity to study abroad. She enrolled in a mini writing course taking place in

Belize. I wanted to go with her to help her get through the airports, stay steady, and keep her safe. I did not get to go. She went on her own and loved it—the people she met, the places she visited, and the mountains she conquered. They offered special excursions to visit ancient ruins, zip-line, and explore caves. Her lack of balance and inability to steadily maneuver some things kept her from zip-lining, but she enjoyed the rest. She climbed to the top of the Mayan ruins of Xunantunich, a miracle in itself. She explored ancient ruins inside a cave from a small boat where she wore a headlight to see. She danced with Mayan dancers and wore the customary clothing. She made chocolate by crushing cocoa beans, a new discovery of hers. This was probably the longest we had ever been apart. I am so thankful that God follows and protects her wherever she goes.

She was able to travel to Washington, DC, and share her story as she introduced the wonderful programs Texas A&M has to offer. I was able to travel with her and watch her talk to others so confidently. She was so passionate about wanting to let those with lived experiences know they can do as much as they want to do.

Thoughts from Shelbi
"I could hardly believe that I got accepted into Texas A&M University! What a miracle! I knew I had worked hard, but so many people were letting me know how difficult it is to be accepted into that university. College was amazing! It was a struggle, but worth every tear and anxious thought. When I finally had a professor who understood how I could relay my knowledge, I was on top of the world. It was so disappointing as I failed test after test. I studied. I memorized. I knew it all. I could not pick the right multiple-choice question, no matter how much I knew. Finding my voice to ask for help and alternate ways of testing paid off. I had some fantastic teachers, and I thank God for putting them right where I needed them to be. The day I received my ring was amazing! I did not have to try on my mom's ring anymore. I have my own!

Getting involved in speaking to and training others with lived experiences was a dream come true. I always wanted to give back."

Promise Keeper is one of my favorite names for God. He never tells you wrong, or deceives you, or tries to trick you. God is faithful and always true to His Word. During this time in our lives, we were able to see many of His promises come true. Parents of children with lived experiences need to believe what I said. Your child cannot be truly independent until you give them true independence. Be careful not to enable them to be disabled. They can do more than you ever imagined.

On top of Xunantunich in Belize

Studying abroad in Belize

Gold medal for swimming in the Special Olympics

8

LIGHT IN THE DARKNESS

The Lord who is present. He never leaves you. He never forsakes you. He is with you forever. He is your best friend, who never betrays you.

—THE LORD IS THERE EZEKIEL 48:35 (NIV)

On Shelbi's twenty-fourth birthday, she had her eyes set on graduation. One of her presents was a Texas A&M graduation cap and gown. She and I love to celebrate our birthdays for the full month. We went to the movies, saw a theater production, and drove to Galveston to spend a few hours on the beach. Shelbi had homework to do, and she did so on the beach. February ended, and we began to count down the weeks, days, and hours until graduation. May 7, 2020, would be here before we knew it.

Her last spring break as a student began like all the others. We headed to Kari's house and enjoyed four fun-filled days with family.

We rode a rail into downtown Austin, toured the Capitol, and ate at a fancy restaurant. Shelbi had a school assignment to spend four hours participating in a leisure activity and take pictures to keep a record of what took place. From all that you have read about Shelbi, you probably know that her family means everything to her. Her most peaceful moments are found in spending time with them. On this day, all eleven of us were together. The train ride was pure enjoyment since it was a first in Austin. It brought back memories of riding the subway in New York, minus the darkness. It was a beautiful day. We walked a couple of miles to see the Capitol. I love this building, and Shelbi knows how much I enjoy seeing it. It never gets old to me. She loves to see her family together, sharing stories and making memories. We concluded the day with a music fest in Kari's backyard. Shelbi danced and sang with her niece and nephews. Her leisure assignment was completed. That was the easiest homework she had ever done. We went to bed late that night and thanked God for a wonderful day and a great family.

Our last public outing was to the Alamo Drafthouse where we watched a movie with her dad and nephews. Shelbi loves to go to this movie house. Being served a full meal, snack, and dessert while watching your favorite movie is especially satisfying. She ordered her favorite wings, and the boys ordered popcorn, a hot dog, and pizza. Her dad and I enjoyed the leftovers. Shelbi sat between Landon and Logan and loved every moment. Kari and Jeremy were celebrating their thirteenth wedding anniversary while we were at the movies. This was our last night at Kari's house. The time spent with family was wonderful, and as we left their house, we had no idea that our normal way of life was about to change drastically.

The excitement and joy of beginning the last half of Shelbi's last semester at Texas A&M soon faded with a simple, yet profound, email. Spring break was to be extended for one week! What a wonderful idea, except the reason for the extension was tragic. The coronavirus had reached the United States. COVID-19 quickly became a pandemic, and the plans we had made earlier quickly dissolved. There were more emails, more tears, and more frustration as the virus spread. No on-campus classes would take place for the rest of the semester. Everything would be completed online. Shelbi realized she would never again step foot in a classroom as a student at the university. She was overwhelmed with sadness. She had already imagined going to school on the very last day. Her outfit was going to be brand-new. She and I had planned a day of celebrating. That day would not come.

The next email was worse. Graduation was canceled! Her diploma would be mailed to her. We were astonished. This could not be! We had never experienced anything like this. Even through these awful moments, God shone in the darkness. Shelbi found optimism and quickly realized this was not the end of the world—or was it?

Fear crept into the world, and we found ourselves unable to purchase toilet paper, disinfectant soap, and wipes. The shelves were empty as people went crazy buying supplies for their families. Churches canceled services when told to not have gatherings of more than ten people. Soon, restaurants and many businesses closed or shut down. All the schools were closed indefinitely, and people were faced with finding care for their children while they worked, if they were fortunate enough to still have jobs. Most employees sent their staff home to work from the confinement of their homes.

The family time that Shelbi enjoyed most was put on hold. Kari and her family were forced to hunker down and stay in Cedar Park. They could not take any chances on exposing Landon to this disease. The uncertainty of how it would affect a child with type 1 diabetes kept them on guard. Our family knows that God does not give us a spirit of fear, but of a sound mind. Whether or not we believed this virus would attack our family did not bring fear. We all knew God would be with each of us. No matter how long we were separated and isolated at home, God was with us. He promises to never leave or forsake us, and Shelbi knew this to be true. She believed that promise through every stage of her life and was fully assured of it now.

The following year forced us to live in a world that was

completely changed. Shelbi had always been energized when she spoke face to face with her audience. She smiled and saw their smiles in return. Masks changed all that. They covered up all those beautiful smiles, and she found herself only seeing them on her laptop. Zoom meetings became a way of life. This technology allowed her to continue training and encouraging others. I watched as she smiled at the laptop. It did not take long for her to gain the same energy. She began to feel just as comfortable on camera as she did in person. We both still preferred in-person meetings but were thankful that we could still teach and get together with others. In fact, due to the virtual meetings, she was able to reach many more people than we ever thought possible.

Shelbi's graduation from A&M was held in our living room. Zoom allowed us to share it with friends and family members. We all watched together as her name was flashed on the jumbotron at Kyle Field. My heart, once again, was breaking and mending at the same time. Dressing in her Texas A&M graduation regalia proved her self-determination. The miracle of that was the icing on the cake. The hard work, the tears, the wonderfully caring professors, and the ones who were not so caring all made that day possible. My Shelbi was graduating from Texas A&M University with honors! She worked through all the noes and cannots and turned them into success.

Shelbi's first job was as a teacher's assistant in a special school for children with lived experiences. During the interview, she was open with sharing all her strengths and weaknesses. She was thrilled to be working with young children to help them be all they could be. In-service began, and Shelbi realized the woman who interviewed and hired her was no longer employed there. She was placed in the class with the youngest children. As the week progressed, Shelbi voiced her concerns about some of the tasks she would be required to do. She also gave ideas on how to adjust those tasks to fit her abilities. For example, instead of lifting a child to a changing table, she could put a mat on the floor and change the diaper. Also, instead of sitting on the floor beside the children, she could sit in a chair near them, in order to get up and down quickly without falling. On Friday, just five days into the job, Shelbi was fired. She was told she could not stay because she could not fulfill the duties of the job in the way they required. Once again, her disability interfered with her dreams. She had moved to Austin, decorated her own apartment, and began a life of true independence. She was crushed. I helped her get out of her apartment lease and moved her back to College Station. She would find an employer that would appreciate her for all her abilities and not deny her work based on her disabilities. However sad and disappointing this was, we soon realized it was for the best. God had other plans for Shelbi during the dark year of COVID.

Shelbi's Views
"Ending my college class days so abruptly was disheartening. I felt so sorry for myself for a little while. I soon realized there was so much more to think about. The world changed almost overnight, and I was fortunate to be where I was. Getting hired at the school in Austin was just what I wanted. I love little children, and I knew I could help them. Losing that job was another disappointment, but God showed me He had other plans. I did graduate from Texas A&M University with a degree in agricultural leadership, with minors in youth development and communications. I also graduated cum laude. Thanks for telling me no and making me determined enough to prove you wrong."

What a time in our lives. I am sure the same goes for each of you. Our way of living in freedom was being stripped away as we were isolated from so many. God had to be the light in the darkness, as He always is. He provided the peace and comfort that was needed during this time of uncertainty.

Last family outing before COVID

Graduation, with Shelbi's name on the jumbotron at Kyle Field

Actual graduation, a year later

9

EL ROI: THE GOD WHO SEES

She gave this name to the Lord who spoke to her: "You are the God who sees me," for she said, "I have now seen the One who sees me."

—GENESIS 16:13 (NIV)

Shelbi was able to purchase her very first car in June 2020. She bought a Ford Edge with every safety measure I could imagine. She has been able to make every payment on her own. She loves proving to me that she can be independent. She also pays for her rent, groceries, gas, and other expenses. I wrote most of this before summer 2020. She applied for an internship to work in Maryland as an advocate for people with disabilities during her final semester of college. This did not happen due to COVID restrictions. I was very glad she was not moving out of Texas.

The reason I am finishing this two years later is that part of this biography was painful to relive in my mind. Remembering the events of her high school years was tough. I was heartbroken for Shelbi, and at the same time, for myself. Some of the people I trusted and loved the most hurt us. I felt deceived, unloved, and rejected. I know now that God was urging me on to a new place, and I did not want to budge. I went to high school in a wonderful small town. I married my high school sweetheart and worked in that same small town during the entire thirty-two years of my career. I loved teaching and being a principal. The students I taught, families I met, and coworkers all meant the world to me. I know that all jobs have their ups and downs. I wanted to change all that for Shelbi and protect her from as many downs as I could.

Another reason I did not finish this book was that I began to care for my mom. She was in an assisted living facility when COVID hit. We were no longer able to see her in person. I could talk to her through the glass door or at her window, but I could not hug her, eat meals with her, or take her out to enjoy the sunshine. In August 2020, we moved her into the house that Shelbi and I share. I thank God for the opportunity I had to have Mom in my home. She walked on her own with the help of a walker. I was able to feed her, talk to her, pray with her, bathe her, and take her for special outings. The time I had with Mom was cut short when she passed away on January 11, 2021. We were all shocked and dismayed. My mom was eighty-nine years old, and I was so blessed to have her in my life for such a long time. The year following her death was filled with each of the stages of grief. According to recent studies, the number of stages changed from five to seven, and each of them is real. My family was extremely supportive as I grieved more than I thought possible. Mom was my number one fan. She was my prayer warrior, and I know she knew just what to pray. My mom always wanted me to write a book and she would love that I finally did! Shelbi played a significant role in loving on her memama every day. She became the activities director for our home and encouraged Mom to do crafts and puzzles and watch movies. Shelbi's goal was to keep Mom out of bed for as long as possible each day.

During Mom's stay at our house, Shelbi was hired by Dr.

Grenwelge of Texas A&M to be the program assistant for the Horticulture Options in Plant Sciences (HOPS) project. The project is a two-semester (approximately thirty-two weeks) training program to provide instruction and support to individuals with disabilities to gain the necessary skills and experiences in work readiness to successfully transition into competitive integrated employment in the horticulture industry. Students have the option to become certified on the state or national level.

This was another miracle for our family. Shelbi was able to enter the workforce under the guidance of a wonderful woman of God. Dr. Grenwelge is an amazing mentor, director, and close friend of mine. She loves Shelbi and has given her the chance to rise above all odds. She was one of the cofounders of the PATHS program Shelbi attended in 2014. This new project has the same purpose but with opportunity for horticulture certification.

I cannot say that her job is easy or without obstacles. Shelbi has had to experience a lot of mental and physical uphill battles. Her passion for advocating for others is so strong that she takes it personally when they are hurt or struggling. She wants them to see what she sees and know that it takes hard work to succeed, but it is all worth it. She wants the other staff members to feel what she feels and love the students like she does. She has learned that each of them do and that is what makes the program work. She is learning every day how to accept others and work with adversity when it comes. She loves teaching the students about professionalism, guiding mentors to push the students toward success, and encouraging each of the students to keep on keeping on. The HOPS project saw its first class of students graduate in May 2022. Shelbi was thrilled to know that this year changed the lives of those students, like PATHS did for her. She prays for and loves each of the students and cannot wait to see how they will soar through life. Her second year as program assistant, teacher, and mentor is off to a great start. This program doubled the number of students. They are all doing a great job. I am the parent liaison for the program. I can encourage and assure parents that allowing their children to experience independence is worth it. They must let them try, fail, and figure out how to make it work. My journey with letting Shelbi go out on her own paved the way for me to be able to help other parents.

I am pretty sure that you can see by now that Shelbi never gives up. She is continually striving to reach as many as she can with her message of hope, love, and courage to self-advocate and live life to the fullest. She is involved in other areas of employment as well as HOPS.

Better Lives is a new organization created to support others to get the lives they want. Jeff Garrison-Tate, her mentor whom she met in 2014, put together a team of wonderful people with the same desires as Shelbi. This team is dedicated to reaching the world with opportunities to be all you want to be. Please visit https://betterlivespcp.com/ to learn more. On May 2, 2022, Shelbi launched her *Shelbi Show*. Shelbi is an amazing speaker. She is naturally drawn to an audience. I know I am her mom, but I have been told this by hundreds of people who have heard her speak. Each person has shared how they feel like Shelbi personally knows them when she is sharing. In training or in giving a speech, she is able to help each person feel special. The *Shelbi Show* is a product of Better Lives and can be accessed by going to that website. Shelbi shares a portion of her story in the first two episodes. All the shows are archived on their website. This job also brought special people into her life. Thank you, to the Better Lives team, for encouraging Shelbi and helping her share her vision. We are looking forward to many more years together.

This show allows Shelbi to share her story, interview others with and without lived experiences, and answer questions about how anyone can live a better life, the life they were meant to live. Lived experience is how we describe someone who has a disability. It can be physical, mental, or emotional. I believe all of us are handicapped in one way or another, but many struggle with how to rise above that. I have been greatly humbled in the past eight years as I've encountered so many individuals who are willing to help kids and adults, like Shelbi, to live better lives. I am even more humbled as I watch those with lived experiences love life, love others, and keep fighting.

This book is only the beginning of Shelbi's journey. She has much more to do and an urgency to help others. As I type these last words, I ask you to pray for her whenever you feel led. Her eyesight is giving her problems. We were sent to a specialist in Houston. He affirmed the change in her peripheral vision and the increasing nystagmus. Our fears about facing more severe eye problems are real, but we know that the same God who saw her through the last twenty-six years will see her through this. She was prescribed glasses, and they seem to help for part of the day. Her driving has also been limited to only times when she is certain she is not tired. The parts of her body affected by SCA8 continue to cause difficulties in her daily life, but her heart has not grown weary. She is still Shelbi. Full of love. Full of life. Her balance is better now, and she can cook many things on her own. She no longer fears dropping a hot pan or cutting herself accidently.

To all the parents, grandparents, siblings, guardians, relatives, and friends, keep praying and expecting miracles. Give support when your family member needs support, catch them when they fall, celebrate their victories, and cry with them when they are hurting.

Shelbi knows the God who sees her. She loves the God who sees her, and she wants others to know Him. Her immediate family prays, loves, and treats Shelbi as if SCA8 does not exist. They all know that it does, but her disease does not define her. Her close friends do the same. Your struggles in life do not define you, either. You were created by God for His glory. He loves you just the way you are. We both know that God is holding Shelbi up all along the way. She and I would love for you to know Him also. I am going to end this with Shelbi's own words of encouragement she uses to close each show.

You are important! You are loved! You matter!

Note from Shelbi That Describes a Typical Day

"To me, independence is being able to make my own choices about daily living. I think about it every day. I want to independently drive my car to work. I want to independently put my shoes on. I want to independently fix my own hair. I want to independently choose what I get to eat or wear. I want to independently choose a job I love and am passionate about.

"I know a lot of people take those choices for granted. They get up, eat breakfast, get dressed, tie their shoes, fix their hair, go to work, and come home and do that routine day after day.

"For me, it is not that easy. I get up and must wait for my eyes to focus, not just waking-up-and-facing-the-day focus, but real focus. It used to only take ten or so minutes, then a little longer, and suddenly, four months ago, it began to take at least two hours.

"I also still cannot successfully tie my shoes. I can tie them, but they do not stay tied, and I do not like how they feel when I tie them.

I can fix my own breakfast, but I must think about what it is. Cooking is not a safe option since my brain and my hands tend to not listen to each other all the time. I can use a microwave and a toaster oven. I have tried to find all the helpful tools I could use in the kitchen. Some worked and some did not. I can pour my own milk for cereal, but it takes a lot of thought. Yes, I make messes. Yes, I have to clean them up. But I get to do them.

"Putting on makeup takes me much longer than other people. I can't just rotate a brush or use my hands to rub in foundation quickly. My hands have their own special way of moving, and I must go with their flow. Mascara is a whole different story and is very seldom worn.

"I can brush my hair. If I did it my mom's way, I would wear it down every day, but I like it up. Because I like things a certain way, I have made myself ask for help. I hate asking for help. I never want to admit I can't do it all by myself, but asking for help is actually much more effective than not.

"I have friends at work who will put my hair up and/or tie my shoes, if needed. I ask for help in carrying heavy objects, or even just carrying my coffee from the break room to my office.

"So, now I am dressed, hair fixed or not, shoes tied or not. Now earrings; do you know how small the backs of earrings are? Almost every single day, I drop the back of one or both of my earrings. I spend the next ten or fifteen minutes looking for it, and then I try again. I know I do not have to wear earrings, but I want to, so it is worth it for me. Necklaces—and those little clasps—enough said!

"Then—praise the Lord—I get to drive. I was twenty-four before I was able to take and pass that test. It took that long for my neurologist and ophthalmologist to agree, and for me to get the nerve up to try it out.

But I get to drive; that is also true independence for me.

"Every day, I sit in the driver's seat. I have an automatic seat memory that places it where I need it to be, but my eyes must adjust to make sure the mirrors are correct. I can touch the pedals comfortably. It takes me a while to just turn it on. I also have to make sure my eyes are focused. (Yes, I do make the decision not to drive when my eyes are not focusing. Aren't you thankful for that?) This is a new obstacle that I am still adjusting to. I am now limited to when I can drive, but I am not going to let that get me down. I still get to drive, and drive I will, as long as I can.

"I am thankful for every day. It is not easy, but I get to do it. No one gets to make those choices for me."

He is the God who sees. He sees it all. He knows it all. He is all. Thank you, God, for seeing who Shelbi was to become. Thank you for continuing to show me what you see in her.

First car!

Enjoying work at TAMU

Shelbi with her memama

10

THE LORD, OUR BANNER

Moses built an alter and called it The Lord is my Banner.

—EXODUS 17:15 (NIV)

The Lord is our banner. This chapter contains notes or letters from our family, friends, and others who have fulfilled this verse for Shelbi. It has been said that it takes a village to raise a child, and I know this to be completely true. Shelbi and I would not be where we are today without the love, support, and prayers that have surrounded us. I have been blessed to have people I could lean on during these times of heartbreak, anger, and uncertainty. Raising Shelbi has been challenging but very rewarding. Most children leave home at the age of eighteen. Shelbi is still very much a part of my life. The extra years have proved to be monumental in allowing Shelbi the time she needed to become truly independent. Please read each note carefully to understand how Shelbi lives life and lives it to the fullest. Shelbi is living her best life. She is experiencing more physical difficulties and faces emotional and mental challenges daily. She also knows she can. She can face the day. She can face tomorrow. She can. That is my heart's desire for my beautiful Shelbi.

From Daddy
"My She-She. Shelbi got this name from Landon when he was two years old. He could not say Shelbi, so he called her She-She. Shelbi came along at a perfect time in my life. Our other two daughters were twelve and nine when she was born. It seems we had two separate lives with our kids because of the gaps in ages. Ashley and Kari were taught to help with cows and horses. They were also avid drivers and could run tractors. They played sports and were involved in many activities. They had lots of friends who spent many hours at our house. I am saying all this because, when Shelbi came along, she had to fit the mold of our busy schedules of living life.

"Church was always where the girls sang, participated in plays, and went to church camp. I just took it for granted that Shelbi would fall in line. I did not know how literal that would be. She was always a happy baby. Her sisters helped a lot and played with her. She was their doll in real-life form. We did not know before she could walk how things were going to go so differently. Shelbi's crawling and walking were slower than most, and we noticed her head would tilt to the left when she watched TV. Then the trying to walk and the falling began. This was something we knew was not right, since her sisters had never showed any signs of problems. Even through all the doctor visits, and discovering more and more about her symptoms, she was growing up and was as active as any child. I remember Ruth and I talking about when Shelbi would be able to talk and tell us what she was feeling about what was going on. Little did we know, Shelbi was already compensating with eyesight issues, balance issues, and other difficulties.

"This was when I knew this little girl was special. God did not make a mistake when He created Shelbi. We only had our normal to compare to. Knowing that I passed the gene that caused all this was something I had to deal with. Still, I want my She-She, even with SCA8. She has more determination than anyone you could know. The blessing she is to me and everyone she meets can only be from the many miracles that we have witnessed over the years. I know the trials in life I go through pale when compared to what Shelbi goes through daily.

"This is real-life stuff that you read about other people going through in books and movies. When it is one of your own children, you want to fix the problems or take that child's place. If we had to pick a disease or problem for our child to have, what would we pick? What helped me through all the falling, and not learning to ride a bike like her sisters, was that God had other plans for her life. I am very proud of Shelbi and how she keeps moving forward, even with all the noes she heard and still hears from time to time. I must realize that God wanted His "normal" for her life, not mine. There is a lot more I could say, but I want you, the reader, to get to know her. You will be able to follow her on the many jobs she has and the lives she is touching. This is her story, and it continues."

From Her Sister, Ashley
"I still remember the evening my parents told us that we were going to have a baby. I was eleven years old, and a new baby was something I had wanted for years. We went to the hospital with my mom while she was in labor, and we were there through the process of Shelbi being born. I can still see her little, squishy face. I remember thinking, *This is my baby sister.* I looked at her for what seemed like hours, and I couldn't find one imperfection. She was perfect in every way. And that has proved true, day after day. She was an easy, content baby who slept when she needed to sleep, ate when she needed to eat, and she laughed and played as is expected of a baby. She used to turn her head to the side to look at people. We made jokes like, "She's just made that way," not thinking that this was the beginning of a diagnosis that would

take years to uncover. When she began to try to walk, we knew that something wasn't quite right. She fell often, and she fell hard. As a toddler, she didn't catch herself when she fell, so she broke her nose several times from falling. There were many times when she ran into walls and furniture in our home, a very familiar place. It was like she didn't even see the things she was about to run into. I remember going to the therapies with my mom for Shelbi when she was little, to work on her balance and hand-eye coordination. I remember all of the doctor appointments, and disappointment after disappointment, because what seemed to be the answer always turned out to be wrong. I think, when we finally got a diagnosis, it gave us all permission to accept what was truly going on and begin the knowledge of the developmental delays that would take place in her life. However, Shelbi has never been defined by her disability. From the time she was very small, any time she entered a room, joy and sweetness were present. She was my running buddy. She and I are twelve years apart, so by the time she was aware that I was leaving and going places, she would ask to come with me. Even on the rare occasions when I would say, no, my friends would override my no, and sure enough, Shelbi came along. After all, she wasn't just my baby, she was everyone's baby.

"I moved away for college when she was only six years old. My time at home with Shelbi was fun and free and playful. When I thought I was too old to dress up for Halloween, I dressed up because Shelbi asked me to. When I thought I was too old to carve pumpkins, I still carved pumpkins because Shelbi asked me to. When I didn't believe in Santa anymore, Shelbi never knew that. Having Shelbi in my life meant a daily dose of joy and adventure, whatever that might be. I was big into theater, and Shelbi and I never failed to scare mom with some theater slaps or makeup that made Shelbi look like she had taken a good tumble. As Shelbi began to grow up, I would hear about the difficulties she was facing. I would hear about the hard times at school. It wasn't her physical disability that she had a hard time with, it was people's opinions of her disability and the way she was treated that gave her the hard time. As her oldest sister, I wanted to tell everyone who hurt her exactly what I thought. But I didn't. Shelbi didn't need someone to go talk to the other people, because there will always be people with opinions and doubts and negative comments because someone doesn't fit their idea of who they think a person should be. Shelbi needed me to continue to love and encourage and lift her up, no matter what it was that she was facing or being told, once again, that she couldn't do.

"Having Shelbi as a sister has increased my awareness of a world where disabled people do not have what they need in order to function in public. There are many times when I would pay attention to the place we were in and notice that there was no way that Shelbi could be a part of certain events or do the things that kids her age were doing. And that wasn't because of Shelbi, but because our society expects an ideal of perfection. Everywhere Shelbi went, she exuded light and love, and people flocked to her presence. Shelbi has taught me more than I would have learned otherwise. She has taught me to not only see a disabled person, but also to stop and take the time to explore what I can learn from my time around that person. She has taught me that, with perseverance, anything can be accomplished. She has taught me that when someone says, "You can't," you just keep trying until you show them that you can. Shelbi has taught me that the words I say can have a lasting impact on someone's view of themselves, and so, even as a thirty-nine-year-old woman, before I speak, I pause and think, *Will this be something that will negatively affect this person?* She has taught me that you have no idea what someone has had to overcome just to be sitting beside you in the classroom in college. Having a sister like Shelbi is something I wouldn't change for anything in the world. Shelbi is brave, loving, forgiving, and unstoppable. I cannot wait to continue to watch her flourish and accomplish every dream that comes her way. Whether she is standing on her own two feet or is held up by the support of others, she will be making a difference and changing lives."

From Her Sister, Kari

"So what was it like having Shelbi as my little sister growing up with a disease I knew nothing about? I'll tell you this: it was normal because I didn't know anything different. I was fifteen years old when Shelbi was diagnosed, and I didn't understand, but I feel as though I didn't want to. Two reasons ... if I knew more about it, I'd worry ... and if I knew more about it, I'd worry. Yes, you read that twice. You see, I knew Shelbi was my baby sister, the one I had always wanted and hoped for, and she was beyond perfect in my eyes. To see her with any flaw was just ... it just wasn't what I wanted. Not that her diagnosis is a flaw, but her diagnosis has many negative moving parts, and I refused to let that define her. You see, I'm ten years older than she is. I was her protector from mean little friends who weren't nice to her. I was her protector when she was walking up and down the stairs, making sure her hand was held. I am still her protector as she makes young adult decisions from boys to clothes to TikTok videos. You see, growing up with a baby sister with this disease ... it means nothing, and it means everything. It means she's special. She's stronger than any of us. She doesn't know how to give up, it's just not an option. Growing up with someone as amazing as Shelbi means I have a hero in my baby sister. I have a constant I can always count on to bring out the best in life. She doesn't care that I laugh at how she says "girl" or "world"; she laughs with me, and we laugh about how I say "light" or "bright." We are from Texas! Who doesn't have an accent here? Am I right? Growing up with Shelbi means we do all we can to make sure she is taken care of. Recently, I joined a company because I heard they help with pain and balance. Shelbi has her balance back because of VoxxLife. She wears a Liberty patch that instantly helps her balance, strength, stamina, and so much more! I would go through everything I've ever been through with all the other ridiculous companies I have joined to get to this point of finding something that truly makes a difference for not only Shelbi but for many others around the world. You can purchase these patches from Shelbi, just reach out to her and find out. Growing up with Shelbi was not awkward; our parents are beyond incredible and have played a huge part in her success. Growing up with Shelbi was not hard; she's my baby sister. Granted, I was the baby for ten years, but her coming along completed our family in all the right ways. Shelbi and her special genetics are just what our family needed. She has taught me more than any education ever has or will. Watching her fight for her life inspires me to never give up. There is no road Shelbi cannot travel. I'll be there every step of the way, snapping pics and laughing our way through life. Thank you for being the most incredible human I have ever met, Shelbi Ann! To know her is to love her. If you don't love her, well, it's because you haven't met her!"

From Aunt Eve
"I remember feeling the worry over Shelbi grow in her junior or senior year of high school. There were other family medical events that year that Ruth wanted/needed to be involved with, and she was also still parenting her minor, Shelbi. I saw Shelbi frequently that year, often after a long day of not only school, but after long drives home from a medical facility while her mom cared for this other loved one. Ruth often shared with me the concerns for how hard Shelbi was working on her schoolwork but was ultimately feeling unsuccessful, how even the simple acts of chewing and swallowing had become chores for Shelbi. We were so very worried and sad. What would her life be like? Was there hope? Ruth had been told she would never drive a car. (She couldn't even safely ride a bike!) She would deteriorate to the point of needing a wheelchair (and worse, which was unspeakable). Ruth and Ronald put rails and ramps in their home, preparing for the inevitable. And then, months later, Ruth talked about the program at Texas A&M. Was it too good to be true? Then Ruth was dropping her off in College Station and crying but trying to be strong. 'Am I doing the right thing? I don't want her to feel I have abandoned her!' Ruth stayed in town so she could be available 'just in case.' And then time passed, and Shelbi was graduating from this program. Then Shelbi enrolled

in A&M. *What?* Then Shelbi got her driver's license. *Incredible!* There were many other wow moments, but after a while, we saw that God had made something beautiful out of this bad diagnosis, as only He can.

"I have a child with a congenital heart defect. I have experienced the oppression of a limiting diagnosis and disappointing results from diagnostic procedures. Ruth took that lifetime of facts, lived alongside them, advocated for Shelbi from her heart, and learned and grew with undying *hope* for better. We all say Ruth is like the Ruth of the Bible who stayed with her mother-in-law after losing her own husband, pledging her life to a woman whom she had grown to love, saying, "Where you go, I will go." Through this beautiful act of humility and selflessness, God brought about (in both instances) a future no person could imagine, as is His way. Ruth and Shelbi give witness to the possibilities of what can happen when someone truly gives their life for another and lives for the betterment of that person, over their own needs, seeking God in all things."

I can do all things through Christ who strengthens me.
—Philippians 4:13

From Uncle John
"Happy birthday!"

From Cheryl Grenwelge
"Shelbi, it has been wonderful to watch you grow into the wonderful woman you are today, and I have been so blessed and honored to have been a part of your journey. I look forward to the years ahead and the miracle of you fulfilling every dream. Love always!"

From Pastor Jimmy
"Shelbi is one of the most remarkable young ladies I have ever met. She is a wonderful Christian young lady who walks by faith and not by sight. She has overcome so many obstacles in her life and

continues to maintain such a positive attitude, and it all stems from her tremendous faith in the Lord Jesus Christ. I am excited about what God has in store for her, and I pray He continues to bless and watch over her."

From Randy Consford

"I remember the first time I met Shelbi. It was at one of the Texas gatherings. She had not yet graduated from Texas A&M, and she was determined she would. I was impressed by her spunk, her smile, and her effervescent personality. I knew she could do anything she put her mind to. Over the years, I have seen her several times, and in the last year, we became coworkers. Every team needs a Shelbi to brighten the day and our meetings, even if she is an Aggie. It is safe to say that even a Longhorn can coexist with Shelbi!"

From Uncle Doug

"Shelbi, as your life has unfolded, I have watched the true hand of God unfold parts of life that I marvel at … you are truly a miraculous work of the Most High God."

From Cara

"You are amazing at what you do! Continue to climb those mountains and leave your name!"

From Alyssa Weichert

"Watching Shelbi live her life like nothing can stop her has been such an inspiration. No matter what comes across her path, with the love of her family, friends, and Jesus Christ, she always finds a way to overcome and thrive from her experiences."

From Landon

"Shelbi is a great aunt, and I love her so much. She pushes me to be a lot better and not to give up, just as she never has."

From Lydia
"Shelbi is an amazing aunt and always tries to make everyone happy and get what they want. She is a very good role model, and I want to love people the same way she does."

From Sam
"Shelbi is an amazing aunt and a very good, inspirational person. She always gives me what I want. I love you, Shelbi."

From Daniel
"I love having my aunt Shelbi. I've watched her struggle and overcome again and again. I am amazed at all she does. She loves me and all her family."

From Angelia
"Shelbi is a sweet, kind, and loving person, and she has such a good heart."

From Tammy Costlow
"Shelbi is someone who touches your heart and inspires you every time you are around her. She has this presence that makes you smile. She has a sense of humor that keeps you laughing. Despite all of her challenges, she has never once accepted no or can't as an answer on her life's journey. I consider myself very lucky to have Shelbi Davenport in my life!"

From Neile
"Shelbi is probably one of the most positive people that I know. She always has a smile on her face, always is willing to help with anything asked, and is a great listener. She always makes a point to tell everyone hi and give everyone hugs. She is always a breath of fresh air on a bad day!"

From Stan and Debbie Ortner, Pastor and Wife of First Baptist Church of Bremond, Texas

"We are Shelbi's biggest old-timer fans and complete supporters of all that Shelbi does! We're behind-the-scenes prayer warriors for our sweet Shelbi. We have known Shelbi all of her life. We have heard about and watched all of her struggles in life. Despite all that she and her family have gone through, the Spirit of the Lord has shown Himself every step of the way. Shelbi has always been a great example to us on how to face difficulties. Just give them to Jesus, and come out on the other side a strong witness for Him. Shelbi has been a strong reminder to us that all things are possible with Christ. If anyone tells her she can't do something, she will prove them wrong! She is a fighter and a warrior all wrapped up in a sweet, little body with a sweet, confident voice that gives God all the glory. She has helped us so many times on mission trips and in our church. A true servant and hard worker that God will reward with rich blessings. She is blessed with a wonderful family that has been by her side every step of the way. The impact that Shelbi has had in people's lives will be felt on this earth for many years and eternally in Heaven. Shelbi is as close as we know to being an angel. What's amazing is that she doesn't know it or feel that way at all. That's what makes her so exceptional."

From Her Aunt Martha

"Shelbi, you shine in everything you do, pushing through the hard to find the satisfaction of achieving what seems impossible to many. Watching your mom be your biggest cheerleader, encourager, counselor, and teacher proves we were never meant to be alone. We need each other. You received her help when needed. That is humility in its highest form. You've set such a good example to so many, including myself, to never forget the help of others. Also, to not give up on our dreams, and to think beyond them.

"What I admire the most is your love for your Father Creator and Savior Jesus Christ, your dependence on them for your wisdom and strength, and even comfort, in the most difficult challenges. Also, your boldness in sharing this truth with others, giving the glory to God, the author and perfecter of your faith.

This verse is what I know to be true for you:

Being confident of this very thing, that He which hath begun a good work in you will perform it until the day of Jesus Christ.
—Philippians 1:6 (NLT)

"I am so proud of God's work in you. You've only just begun. Blessings of joy, my dear niece!"

From Amy Howard
"You make lemonade out of lemons. You bring sunshine to a rainy day. You're quiet when life is loud, and you speak up for those who cannot speak for themselves. You've led the way to make possible what was once impossible for so many. Keep paving the way and driving down the road that helps others find their dreams."

From Aunt Becky
"Simple, uncomplicated grace has filled the steps of your life. With that, you demonstrate to the world the same. When others have said, you can't, you have said, 'I can.' I love you, sweet niece."

From Ray and Emily
"Shelbi, we love you. You are living proof that the Lord hears and answers prayers. Always wishing you the best."

From Uncle Danny and Aunt Cindy
"Shelbi, you have inspired us to be more than we think we are capable of. We're so proud of all you have accomplished and will continue to accomplish. You are God's gift to our family, and we love you very much."

From Sherry Lagrone
"Since the day Shelbi was born, we all knew this baby girl with beautiful blue eyes was going to change the world. And she has, yes, the naysayers were wrong. She should be in the Olympics because no one can compete as hard as she has. She has fallen and has shrugged off words and diagnoses that would make most people give up. But not Shelbi! She will fight to the end to prove that, with love from family and friends and Jesus Christ as her guide, she will make her mark on this world. Oh, never mind, she already has!"

From Michelle McCoy and Hayley
"We met Shelbi in 2012, and she has changed our lives forever. Shelbi is an inspiration to all who know her. Although Shelbi has faced many challenges, they haven't stopped her from achieving her goals. Shelbi is a sweet and genuine soul who shares her love with everyone who crosses her path. She has a contagious smile that makes it so that you, too, can't help but smile when you are around her. She is a very compassionate person who sees the good in all people. To know her is to love her. We have been very blessed to know Shelbi and to still have her as a part of our lives!"

From Alyssa (Ortner) Craig
"You have been such an inspiration in my life. All the light and laughter you bring to everyone you encounter is unmatched. I am honored to be your friend. Thank you for always being there for me when I need someone to lean on. I can only hope that I can offer you a glimpse of the friendship you give to me.

"You are doing great! I am so proud of all you have done, and that you choose to inspire those around you. I am always learning from you and trying to be more like you. Thank you for being a role model to me and so many others.

I love you so, so much!"

From Elisa Anaya

"Shelbi has to be the sweetest, kindest, most loving person I have ever met. I remember first meeting Shelbi at her sister's house while I was babysitting her niece and nephews. We hit it off right away, and that's when our friendship began. Fast-forward to today, and I consider Shelbi one of my best, closest friends who I can always rely on. If anyone knows Shelbi, you know that her life hasn't always been easy, but that has not in any way stopped her from achieving her goals. Her disability has not disabled her but rather has enabled her to live her life out to its full potential! I am also a witness of how she points everything back to Jesus and truly lives out the gospel in every area of her life. Her faith in Jesus has absolutely strengthened my own faith, and I know many others. The Lord has already worked in her life in so many ways, and I cannot wait to see what else He has planned for her! I continually aspire to have her strength, faith, and hope. I love you, Shelbi, and I am beyond grateful for the Lord giving me a friend and role model like you! I am so excited to continue walking alongside you in this life! I love you so much."

From Lea Ann Stasney (Blinn Professor)

"Faith. One simple word. And it's a *big word*!

"Thank you for the incredible opportunity to watch your *faith* in yourself as you marched right into my classes and rocked them.

"I *saw* more *faith* in you than I have ever seen in one student.

"I *saw faith* as you faced and tackled the obstacles that college has to offer.

"I *heard faith* in your voice when you stopped by my office to visit, to discuss work, to talk about your plans, and just to visit for the sake of visiting.

"I *knew* you had more than enough *faith* in yourself to succeed.

"From our first meeting, I *believed* right along with you that you would succeed.

"Thank you for the incredible gift of your friendship. Thank you for reminding me of the importance of *faith*!"

WORDS TO THINK ABOUT

As I said throughout the book, Shelbi wants others to live the life of freedom she has found. She knows this freedom comes from her faith in Jesus Christ. She wants each of you to have the opportunity to know Him as she does.

The following verses were special to her when she began to learn about who Jesus is.

> For all have sinned and fall short of the glory of God.
> —Romans 3:23 (NIV)

> For the wages of sin is death, but the gift of God
> is eternal life in Christ Jesus our Lord.
> —Romans 6:23 (NIV)

> But God demonstrates his own love for us in this:
> While we were still sinners, Christ died for us.
> —Romans 5:8 (NIV)

> If you declare with your mouth, "Jesus is Lord," and believe in
> your heart that God raised him from the dead, you will be saved.
> —Romans 10:9 (NIV)

For God so loved the world that he gave his one and only Son, that whoever believes in him shall not perish but have eternal life.
—John 3:16 (NIV)

Therefore, since we have been justified through faith, we have peace with God through our Lord Jesus Christ.
—Romans 5:1 (NIV)

Therefore, there is now no condemnation for those who are in Christ Jesus.
—Romans 8:1 (NIV)

For I am convinced that neither death nor life, neither angels nor demons, neither the present nor the future, nor any powers, neither height nor depth, nor anything else in all creation, will be able to separate us from the love of God that is in Christ Jesus our Lord.
—Romans 8:38–39 (NIV)

This is a special psalm I want to share as a final closing:

Praise the Lord, my soul; all my inmost being, praise his holy name.

Praise the Lord, my soul, and forget not all his benefits—who forgives all your sins and heals all your diseases, who redeems your life from the pit and crowns you with love and compassion, who satisfies your desires with good things so that your youth is renewed like the eagle's. The Lord works righteousness and justice for all the oppressed. He made known his ways to Moses, his deeds to the people of Israel:

The Lord is compassionate and gracious, slow to anger, abounding in love.

He will not always accuse, nor will he harbor his anger forever.

He does not treat us as our sins deserve or repay us according to our iniquities.

For as high as the heavens are above the earth, so great is his love for those who fear him; as far as the east is from the west, so far has he removed our transgressions from us. As a father has compassion on his children, so the Lord has compassion on those who fear him; for he knows how we are formed, he remembers that we are dust.

The life of mortals is like grass, they flourish like a flower of the field; the wind blows over it and it is gone, and its place remembers it no more. But from everlasting to everlasting the Lord's love is with those who fear him, and his righteousness with their children's children—with those who keep his covenant and remember to obey his precepts. The Lord has established his throne in heaven, and his kingdom rules overall. Praise the Lord, you his angels, you mighty ones who do his bidding, who obey his word. Praise the Lord, all his heavenly hosts, you his servants who do his will. Praise the Lord, all his works everywhere in his dominion. Praise the Lord, my soul.

—Psalm 103 (NIV)

Thank you for reading this book. I hope it leaves you with feelings of encouragement and determination to live your best life.

Shelbi and her mom

Printed in the United States
by Baker & Taylor Publisher Services